VGM Opportunities Series

# OPPORTUNITIES IN
# GOVERNMENT
# CAREERS

# Neale J. Baxter

Revised by
**Mark Rowh**

Foreword by
**Larry E. Naake**
Executive Director
National Association of Counties

 **VGM Career Books**

**Library of Congress Cataloging-in-Publication Data**

Baxter, Neale J.
    Opportunities in government careers / Neale J. Baxter; revised by Mark Rowh;
foreword by Larry E. Naake. Rev. Ed.
        p.   cm. — (VGM Opportunities series)
    ISBN 0-658-01048-4 (hardcover)
    ISBN 0-658-01049-2 (paperback)
    Notes: Rev. ed. of: Opportunities in state and local government careers.
Chicago, Ill.: VGM Career Horizons, 1993.
    Includes bibliographical references.
        1. Civil service positions—United States.   2. Civil service positions—United
States—States.   3. Local government—Vocational guidance—United States.

JK716 .B386  2001
351.73'023—dc21

                               00-68501
                                 CIP

**Cover photograph copyright © PhotoDisc**

First published as *Opportunities in State and Local Government Careers* by VGM
Career Horizons in 1993

Published by VGM Career Books
A division of The McGraw-Hill Companies.
4255 West Touhy Avenue, Lincolnwood (Chicago), Illinois 60712-1975 U.S.A.

Printed in the United States of America
International Standard Book Number:  0-658-01048-4 (hardcover)
                                          0-658-01049-2 (paperback)

1   2   3   4   5   6   7   8   9   0   LB/LB   0   9   8   7   6   5   4   3   2   1

# CONTENTS

# ABOUT THE AUTHOR

Neale Baxter was managing editor of *The Occupational Outlook Quarterly,* a general career information magazine published by the U.S. Department of Labor. He has also served with the U.S. Army overseas and worked for state and local governments. He has written for *Career World* and the *Monthly Labor Review* and teaches at George Mason University.

Mr. Baxter received his bachelor's degree from Manhattan College, his master's from Purdue University, and his Ph.D. from the University of North Carolina at Chapel Hill. He lives in Virginia.

This edition has been thoroughly revised and updated by Mark Rowh.

# FOREWORD

One of the most popular pastimes of modern society is complaining about "the government." After all, we live in a free society, and everyone has the right to complain about virtually anything. As a society we also have many problems, and we look to government to solve them. Yet governing is complex, and on any public issue, you'll find varying opinions and differing levels of interest.

Notwithstanding such problems, an objective look at government reveals its undeniable importance. Without government, there would be no laws or means of enforcing them. There would be no social programs for the public good and no assurance that people have basic inalienable rights. Without government, there would be no publicly funded schools, libraries, or highway systems, not to mention countless other beneficial programs.

Fortunately, we do have a highly organized governmental system. Within the various agencies and other units of government, millions of people are employed. In fact, federal, state, provincial, county, and other local governments rank among the largest employers in the United States and Canada.

In many cases, the men and women who hold jobs in government enjoy truly challenging careers. Their work can be important in making sure that government agencies and programs fulfill their goals. This might involve such diverse work as helping in the development of national legislation, overseeing a county's economic development efforts, or providing leadership for a small town.

Can you picture yourself developing a public relations program for a state highway department? Or working in a county department that preserves the environment or promotes economic development? Or running for public office? Or helping manage a large federal agency? These are just a few examples of roles played by government employees.

In the future, large numbers of new employees will be needed in various areas of government. As present employees retire, and as new programs are created or existing ones expanded, a continuing need will exist for highly motivated workers to pursue government careers.

*Opportunities in Government Careers* presents an overview of the possibilities to be encountered in government employment. If a career in government sounds interesting, you are invited to read further and explore available options. Who knows? Perhaps a career in government awaits you. If so, you can look forward to a job that is likely to play an important role in making life better for fellow citizens.

Larry E. Naake
Executive Director
National Association of Counties

## CHAPTER 1

# INTRODUCTION TO GOVERNMENT EMPLOYMENT

*Teacher, police officer, librarian, social worker*—if you wish to enter one of these occupations, this book is for you, because most of these workers are employed by state and local governments.

*Judge, nurse, word processor, accountant, civil engineer, elected official*—if you wish to follow one of these occupations, this book is for you, too, because federal, state, and local government agencies and departments employ thousands of these workers.

National, state, and local government agencies are major providers of *services.* They provide education, mass transportation, fire protection, health services, and welfare services, as well as the vital service of managing the the government itself. Consequently, they are likely employers for people in occupations such as the following:

| | |
|---|---|
| accountant | extension service specialist |
| building engineer | firefighter |
| building inspector | food service worker |
| coach | forester |
| college and university instructor | health inspector |
| computer programmer, analyst | highway maintenance worker |
| elected official | judge |
| emergency medical technician | land use manager |
| | librarian |
| | nutritionist |

police officer
postal worker
sanitation worker
school principal
sheriff
teacher

urban and regional planner
water and wastewater
    conservation and
    treatment worker
word processor

These governments also employ more people in their own operations than any other industry in the country. As a consequence, thousands of people in occupations such as the following work for them:

accounting clerk
administrative assistant
automotive mechanic
bookkeeper
building engineer
civil engineer
clerical supervisor
clinical lab technician
computer programmer
electrician
file clerk
food services worker
gardener and groundskeeper

guard
heavy equipment operator
lawyer
licensed practical nurse
maintenance worker
nursing aide and orderly
physician
psychiatric aide
recreation worker
registered nurse
social worker
systems analyst
therapist

Altogether, more than 1.8 million people are employed as civilian employees of the federal government. Millions more work for the armed forces and the U.S. Postal Service. Another 7.2 million are employed by state and local governments, not counting the education and hospital sectors. This book is a guide to these jobs. It will introduce you to the scope of state and local government and point out the incentives and drawbacks of a government career.

Much of the book deals with specific occupations in which governments are either the major employer or the employer of thousands of workers. In addition, some other occupations associated with government—city manager, for example—are described. For each of the major occupations, there is information on the nature of the work, what you should bring to the occupation, its rewards, where you can get a job, and where to learn more about the field. For other occupations, at least some information is given on the nature of the work, training required, number of people employed, and—usually—sources of information besides those listed in the appendix material.

The section on *the nature of the work,* which immediately follows the occupation's title, describes the usual duties and work environment of the job, including information on unusual work hours or working conditions.

*What you should bring to this occupation* describes the personal characteristics, aptitudes, skills, experience, and education that make people successful at this kind of work. The kinds of tests applicants must usually take are also indicated, along with the training given to new workers.

*The rewards* deals with salaries and other benefits, such as vacation and sick leaves; it also indicates nonmonetary benefits, such as personal satisfaction or the chances for advancement, and some things to make you think twice about the occupation—the reasons why some workers are dissatisfied.

*Where to find a job* indicates the number of people who work for state and local governments in this occupation, mentioning the usual employing agency when possible. Other sources of employment also are given for many occupations. Information on the job outlook over the next ten years is also given, in cases where projections are available.

The last section, *Where to learn more,* provides the names and addresses of associations of workers in the field and lists periodicals and books that can give you more insight into the occupation. The sources of information listed in the appendix material should also prove useful.

## CHAPTER 2

# THE DIVERSITY OF GOVERNMENT JOBS

Let's begin with the scope of government—its size and major functions.

By any measure, government employment is very large. More than 7 million people worked for state and local governments in 1998, not including the additional millions working in the education and hospital sectors. This places state and local governments among the nation's largest employers (see Table 1). The federal government employs another 1.8 million workers, not including the military and the U.S. Postal Service.

The size of the state and local government labor force varies from place to place, ranging from large states such as California and Texas to small states such as Vermont. Population is the major reason for the differences, but many other factors also come into play. Some variation is due to different needs. Rural areas don't need the same services that large cities do; and if the private sector traditionally provides hospitals or utilities, the state or local government does not have to. But much of the variation is also due to the willingness and ability of the citizens to pay for government services.

At the national level, the three branches of government (legislative, judicial, and executive) are all major employers. About 98 percent of all federal civilian employees (other than postal workers)

**Table 1. Employment of Wage and Salary Workers in State and Local Government, Excluding Education and Hospitals, by Occupation, 1998 and Projected Change, 1998–2008 (employment in thousands)**

| Occupation | 1998 Employment | | 1998–2008 |
|---|---|---|---|
| | NUMBER | PERCENT | PERCENT CHANGE |
| All occupations | 7,152 | 100.0 | 11.8 |
| Service | 2,043 | 28.6 | 19.5 |
| Police patrol officers | 431 | 6.0 | 32.1 |
| Correctional officers | 361 | 5.0 | 37.9 |
| Firefighters | 228 | 3.2 | 5.5 |
| Cleaning and building service occupations, except private household | 124 | 1.7 | 1.7 |
| Personal service occupations | 104 | 1.5 | 10.4 |
| Police and supervisors | 102 | 1.4 | 13.3 |
| Sheriffs and deputy sheriffs | 91 | 1.3 | 34.2 |
| Nursing aides, orderlies, and attendants | 71 | 1.0 | 10.8 |
| Administrative support, including clerical | 1,445 | 20.2 | 1.6 |
| Office clerks, general | 281 | 3.9 | 18.1 |
| Secretaries | 197 | 2.8 | −10.8 |
| Word processors and typists | 111 | 1.6 | −31.2 |
| Office and administrative support supervisors and managers | 103 | 1.4 | 7.7 |
| Bookkeeping, accounting, and auditing clerks | 85 | 1.2 | −9.7 |
| Dispatchers, police, fire, and ambulance | 77 | 1.1 | 6.0 |
| Adjusters, investigators, and collectors | 76 | 1.1 | −3.0 |
| Professional specialty | 1,134 | 15.9 | 18.7 |
| Social workers | 219 | 3.1 | 35.2 |
| Teachers, librarians, and counselors | 128 | 1.8 | 10.6 |
| Recreation workers | 109 | 1.5 | 11.9 |
| Lawyers and judicial workers | 105 | 1.5 | 10.0 |
| Social and human service assistants | 84 | 1.2 | 21.3 |

*(Continued)*

**Table 1. Continued**

| Occupation | 1998 Employment | | 1998–2008 |
|---|---|---|---|
| | **NUMBER** | **PERCENT** | **PERCENT CHANGE** |
| Engineers | 75 | 1.1 | 10.6 |
| Registered nurses | 82 | 1.1 | 10.3 |
| Executive, administrative, and managerial | 936 | 13.1 | 8.4 |
| Inspectors and compliance officers, except construction | 84 | 1.2 | 12.1 |
| Government chief executives and legislators | 79 | 1.1 | 2.8 |
| General managers/top executives | 76 | 1.1 | 7.6 |
| Accountants and auditors | 78 | 1.1 | 3.2 |
| Precision production, craft, and repair | 757 | 10.6 | 8.0 |
| Highway maintenance workers | 143 | 2.0 | 11.2 |
| Blue-collar worker supervisors | 109 | 1.5 | 11.1 |
| Maintenance repairers, general utility | 89 | 1.2 | −10.2 |
| Water and liquid waste treatment plant and system operators | 80 | 1.1 | 12.0 |
| Construction equipment operators | 75 | 1.1 | 11.2 |
| Operators, fabricators, and laborers | 358 | 5.0 | 8.2 |
| Helpers, laborers, and material movers | 166 | 2.3 | 8.4 |
| Motor vehicle operators | 140 | 2.0 | 7.0 |
| Technicians and related support | 316 | 4.4 | 7.3 |
| Health technicians and technologists | 133 | 1.9 | 9.1 |
| Technicians, except health and engineering and science | 94 | 1.3 | 5.6 |
| Engineering and science technicians and technologists | 55 | 0.8 | 10.1 |
| Agriculture, forestry, fishing, and related occupations | 116 | 1.6 | 11.5 |
| Laborers, landscaping, and groundskeeping | 79 | 1.1 | 11.7 |
| All other occupations | 47 | 0.7 | 9.5 |

Provided by the U.S. Department of Labor.

are employed within the executive branch, which includes fourteen executive cabinet departments and more than ninety independent agencies.

## WHAT DO ALL THESE PEOPLE DO?

Given the millions of government workers, you might expect to be hard pressed to answer the question, "What do all these people do?" But the answer is surprisingly easy for almost half of them—they educate us. Education accounts for far more jobs than any other government function. Local governments—usually special school districts—are the major employers of people who work in education, including teachers, administrators, teacher aides, librarians, and school counselors. Other major functions of local governments are providing police and fire protection, hospitals, streets and highways, water, and transit service.

Employees of state governments are not quite as concentrated *by field* as local government workers are, although 30 percent are engaged in higher education. Functions employing at least 5 percent of all state workers are hospitals, highways, correction, and public welfare. This means that state governments employ many college professors, librarians, nurses, psychiatric aides, other medical specialists, engineers, highway construction workers, correction officers or prison guards, social workers, and welfare aides. At the federal level, employees work in areas such as national defense, veterans affairs, treasury and financial affairs, health and human services, transportation, commerce, and housing and urban development.

As you can see, government is a very large industry. But that does not make finding a job easy, primarily because there are so many different employers: scores of federal agencies and departments; 50 states plus 5 territories, Puerto Rico, and the District of Columbia; approximately 3,000 counties; 19,400 municipalities;

16,600 towns; 34,700 special districts; and, finally, 13,700 school districts.

That makes about 87,000 different local governments, or governmental bodies, plus federal governmental units, each of which does its own hiring. And each government may have more than one hiring system. Each state, for example, has an agency similar to the former Civil Service Commission of the federal government that establishes eligibility standards, administers examinations, and maintains registers of eligible applicants. But as many as half the state's employees may be hired according to other procedures. For example, the court system and the legislature are not usually under the civil service system.

Despite the existence of these many different systems, all is not chaos. As shown in the following chapter, many of the benefits and even the disadvantages of government employment are roughly comparable. And many governments follow the same kinds of hiring procedures. Besides, with more than 87,000 potential employers, you have that many more places to find a job.

## FOR WHAT KINDS OF GOVERNMENTS?

State and local governments come in many shapes and sizes. The U.S. Census Bureau conducts an annual survey of government employment. For the survey, it divides governments among the following groups.

- *County.* Organized county governments, called *boroughs* in Alaska and *parishes* in Louisiana.
- *Municipality.* A political subdivision of a county that provides general government services to a concentrated population in a defined geographic area. Municipalities are also called cities, villages, boroughs (except in Alaska), and towns (except in New England, Minnesota, New York, and Wisconsin). Some

municipalities have taken over the entire area of a county or, in the case of New York City, several counties. Among these cities are Anaconda; Anchorage; Baltimore; Baton Rouge; Boston; Butte; Carson City; Columbus, Georgia; Denver; Honolulu; Indianapolis; Jacksonville; Juneau; Lexington, Kentucky; Nashville; New Orleans; Philadelphia; St. Louis; Sitka; and San Francisco. Washington, DC, combines the functions of a city, county, and state government.

- *Township.* A subdivision of a county that provides general government services in a defined geographical area without regard to the concentration of the population. Twenty states use this classification. The governments are called *towns* in New England, New York, and Wisconsin; *plantations* in Maine; and *locations* in New Hampshire.
- *School District.* The census notes that there is a "marked organizational diversity in the types of governmental units that provide for the operation of public schools." School districts that are completely independent of all other local governments are found in forty-five states. Dependent school systems are found in Alaska, Hawaii, Maryland, North Carolina, Virginia, and Washington, DC; the school system is dependent on a local government or the state government. Eleven states have both independent and dependent school systems.
- *Special District.* A government that provides only one or a few related services, which makes them like school districts. The district may be called an *authority*, *board*, or *commission*. Among the services provided by special districts are soil conservation, water, bridges, housing, community development, fire protection, and hospitals. These districts, like school districts, vary enormously in size.

At the federal level, governmental units include executive departments (such as the Department of Defense, Department of

Agriculture, and Department of Labor), independent agencies (such as the General Services Administration, National Aeronautics and Space Administration, and Environmental Protection Agency), and other units.

## THE PAST AND THE FUTURE

The trend since the 1940s has been to fewer and fewer units of state and local government. This trend is most noticeable in the totals for school districts. The decades of the 1940s and 1950s saw a rapid decline in rural and small town districts as people began to recognize the need for broader education programs to meet the challenges of a technological society. The only significant increase has been in the number of special districts.

The decline in the number of units of state and local government does not, however, tell the story of public sector employment. During the second half of the twentieth century, the number of government employees grew substantially, even despite some periodic efforts to reduce the size of government.

The shifts in both the number of units of state and local governments and the number of citizens employed in the public sector can be traced to several factors. First, the increase in population of the United States from about 151 million in 1950 to more than 270 million in 2000 producing greater needs for all services. Second, greater expectations and demands for social services. Third, a trend to return some tax monies to the states rather than continuing federal programs (revenue sharing, block grants, etc.). The overall aging of the population is another factor.

## HOW GOVERNMENTS ARE ORGANIZED

Some governments closely follow the federal organization, that is, all executive functions are directed by a mayor or governor just as the president is in charge of all departments of the national government. More frequently, however, the chief executive does *not* control all departments. In addition to a governor, many states elect an attorney general, commissioner of education, and other officials, each of whom has final authority for a department; this is sometimes referred to as the plural executive system of government. At the local level, legislative and executive functions are often invested in a single body, the board, which makes local government very different from the federal model. Most local governments follow one of four patterns.

- *Mayor-council or elected executive-council:* these governments do resemble the federal system.
- *Council-city manager or commission-county manager:* the council acts as the legislature and hires a professional manager to see to day-to-day administration. The council may also choose a mayor from among its members, but the office is largely ceremonial.
- *Commissioner:* the commissioners as a group exercise legislative functions; each commissioner is also the head of one or more departments; a major or chief administrative officer may be elected separately or chosen by the board from among its members.
- *Town meeting:* a meeting of the electorate or a large number of elected representatives sets policy and chooses a board of selectmen to carry the policies out; the meeting or the board may also hire a professional manager.

## CHAPTER 3

# REWARDS AND FRUSTRATIONS OF GOVERNMENT EMPLOYMENT

The benefits and drawbacks of government employment largely depend on the particular occupation you enter or the individual job you hold. The satisfactions of a teacher, for example, are very different from those of a police officer. Still, some of the pluses and minuses of a government job hold true across many occupations.

## EARNINGS

Generalizing about the pay practices of thousands of different employers is risky. Studies show that one government pays its clerical workers relatively well while its electricians would do better with a private company; another government does just the opposite, paying electricians much better than average and clerical workers less than the going rate.

When asking about salaries, people often request a figure, but they really want to know how one occupation's salary compares with another's. Here are some managerial occupations and average 1998 salaries paid by city governments:

| | |
|---|---|
| City manager | $70,000 |
| Engineer | 59,777 |

| | |
|---|---|
| Chief financial officer | 55,347 |
| Fire chief | 52,645 |
| Personnel director | 50,543 |
| Human services director | 43,332 |
| Purchasing director | 43,255 |

At the federal level, many positions are paid according to the standard General Schedule (GS), with salaries ranging from under $14,000 at the lowest grade to more than $100,000 at the highest (see Table 2). And executive pay levels may go as high as $157,000 or more.

When considering salaries, keep in mind that economic conditions quickly make salary figures out of date, but the relative salaries for different occupations remain more constant. You can use this information when you are offered a salary to help you evaluate the proposal. Here are some considerations to keep in mind in addition to dollar amounts.

- What do private companies pay workers in the occupation? Even if government pays a little less, the other benefits and the security of a government position may make it worthwhile to consider.
- Is the annual salary paid in less than twelve months—as in the case of many teachers? If so, you can correct for distortion.
- Besides salary, do you receive benefits such as housing or meals that lower your cost of living?
- Is the occupation unionized? Union workers tend to be better paid, but they must also pay union dues.

Despite the great number of employers and the many different occupations involved, many government and private-sector employees enjoy comparable fringe benefits. The most common are paid vacation and sick leave, paid holidays, medical insurance, retirement plans, and tuition assistance. Comprehensive data are not

**Table 2. General Schedule (GS) Pay Rates for 2000**

| Grade | Annual Rates for Steps (in dollars) | | | | | | | | | |
|---|---|---|---|---|---|---|---|---|---|---|
| 1. | 13,870 | 14,332 | 14,794 | 15,252 | 15,715 | 15,986 | 16,440 | 16,900 | 16,918 | 17,351 |
| 2. | 15,594 | 15,964 | 16,481 | 16,918 | 17,107 | 17,610 | 18,113 | 18,616 | 19,119 | 19,622 |
| 3. | 17,015 | 17,582 | 18,149 | 18,716 | 19,283 | 19,850 | 20,417 | 20,984 | 21,551 | 22,118 |
| 4. | 19,100 | 19,737 | 20,374 | 21,011 | 21,648 | 22,285 | 22,922 | 23,559 | 24,196 | 24,833 |
| 5. | 21,370 | 22,082 | 22,794 | 23,506 | 24,218 | 24,930 | 25,642 | 26,354 | 27,066 | 27,778 |
| 6. | 23,820 | 24,614 | 25,408 | 26,202 | 26,996 | 27,790 | 28,584 | 29,378 | 30,172 | 30,966 |
| 7. | 26,470 | 27,352 | 28,234 | 29,116 | 29,998 | 30,880 | 31,762 | 32,644 | 33,526 | 34,408 |
| 8. | 29,315 | 30,292 | 31,269 | 32,246 | 33,223 | 34,200 | 35,177 | 36,154 | 37,131 | 38,108 |
| 9. | 32,380 | 33,459 | 34,538 | 35,617 | 36,696 | 37,775 | 38,854 | 39,933 | 41,012 | 42,091 |
| 10. | 35,658 | 36,847 | 38,036 | 39,225 | 40,414 | 41,603 | 42,792 | 43,981 | 45,170 | 46,359 |
| 11. | 39,178 | 40,484 | 41,790 | 43,096 | 44,402 | 45,708 | 47,014 | 48,320 | 49,626 | 50,932 |
| 12. | 46,955 | 48,520 | 50,085 | 51,650 | 53,215 | 54,780 | 56,345 | 57,910 | 59,475 | 61,040 |
| 13. | 55,837 | 57,698 | 59,559 | 61,420 | 63,281 | 65,142 | 67,003 | 68,864 | 70,725 | 72,586 |
| 14. | 65,983 | 68,182 | 70,381 | 72,580 | 74,779 | 76,978 | 79,177 | 81,376 | 83,575 | 85,774 |
| 15. | 77,614 | 80,201 | 82,788 | 85,375 | 87,962 | 90,549 | 93,136 | 95,723 | 98,310 | 100,897 |

available for local governments. However, the practices of the states show the usual benefits offered.

New workers typically get 2 weeks of vacation and 12 to 18 days of sick leave; almost all the states give additional vacation time to workers with more service; 25 or more days a year is the maximum in several states. Most states grant at least 8 paid holidays a year, and many have up to 12 or 13; Hawaii gives 15. The entire cost of medical insurance is paid in some states, while others pay at least part of the cost of medical insurance and in many cases offer some kind of life insurance plan.

Government pensions are often considered generous and most states provide tuition assistance for college. The amount provided and the kinds of courses that may be taken vary widely.

Other frequently mentioned benefits of government jobs are job security and advancement opportunities. Government employment is not guaranteed in bad times, as the teachers in many a shrinking school district can attest. Still, a government is less likely to be affected by temporary economic setbacks than is a private company. This side effect of government employment is especially beneficial in occupations that are prone to high unemployment, such as construction.

As for advancement, government positions often have clearly defined career ladders. Furthermore, in many government agencies, managerial positions are usually held by people who once worked at lower levels of the organization. For example, school administrators are often former teachers in the system; police sergeants and officers almost always come from the patrol ranks.

## DISADVANTAGES

Just as government service offers some solid advantages, it has some disadvantages. The degree to which they bother you is likely to depend on your own personality. One frustration of government work for some is a lack of prestige.

Prestige cannot be held in your hand. It won't help put dinner on the table or T-shirts on your back. But it contributes a great deal to job satisfaction. The prestige of a job cannot be measured very easily, either; yet everyone seems to know that, socially, a doctor is a step above a lawyer, and lawyers outrank accountants. Everyone also seems to know that a doctor in private practice has more prestige than one who works for the government, that a lawyer with a private firm outranks one with the government, and that accountants with private corporations are better thought of than ones who work for the government.

Government jobs, except for those at the very top, are low in prestige. Tell people you work for the government, and they seem forced to say, "I guess you don't work too hard then. You government workers have it made." Usually remarks like that don't mean much, but they are so common that one is bound to hit you on a day when you started work early, skipped lunch, and had to put in some overtime, so that four different projects—all set up by people elected by the person making the remark, in order to serve the person making the remark—could move forward.

Some drawbacks are related to each other. Politicians have a history of appointing people to jobs because the job seeker helped the politician get elected, rather than because the job seeker is qualified. Therefore, the civil service was set up a hundred years ago to make sure that qualified people were hired by the government and that a newly elected politician could not fire all the workers of the opposite political party. One unfortunate result of the need to isolate the civil service from politics is that some marginal workers become entrenched in positions they are no longer fit to hold.

One other drawback of government jobs, despite the conventional wisdom, is that some don't pay well. The GS pay system is fairly rigid. It is the same throughout the country, and when cost-of-living adjustments are given—as they are most years—they are usually a flat percentage increase for all grades and steps. For these reasons, and because of the way occupations are grouped together, some government employees would be better paid by private firms. For example, writer-editors fresh out of college receive relatively high wages in government jobs, but experienced lawyers do not. And federal employees in the South are better paid in relation to their cost of living than employees in the North and Far West. Furthermore, no one who is honest becomes rich in a government job. Government workers do not command the exorbitant incomes of very successful doctors, lawyers, sales representatives, or executives. And even though most government salaries are fairly good, salaries are going down relative to the national average. Representatives, senators, and presidents find it difficult to give a full cost-of-living increase to government workers. They find it easier to complain about the workers, lower their salaries, and then complain some more.

Fringe benefits, too, are sometimes not as good as those found in strongly unionized industries or major corporations. The government's reputation for good fringe benefits is largely based on what it did fifty years ago. Since then, other employers have matched or surpassed them. Two exceptionally good fringe benefits in the government are the policies on sick leave and annual leave, which are extremely generous. However, the government offers no stock options, employee discounts, or Christmas bonuses, all of which can add substantially to a worker's salary (some of the addition being sheltered from taxes). Also, health plans and life insurance policies offered to government workers are sometimes not as good as those available to workers with large, private companies.

Another potential frustration is the inability to measure achievement in terms of profit and loss. When a private company offers goods or services to the public, it can use sales to measure its success. Governments do not sell products on the open market, and government programs rarely have a clear-cut success. No matter how good the schools, no matter how safe the community, no matter how well kept the roads, some citizens will always be found to say that the service should be better or cheaper or both. Politics also has a major effect on government workers, since politicians control the budget and make the final decisions. This can be a disadvantage to those who always want to have the last word on their own work. Furthermore, the same organization controls that provide job security can protect the job of someone you think you should replace. And the explicit promotion procedures can result in advancement that is sure but slow. Nor does the government offer the extremely high salaries and bonuses that a few very successful workers in the private sector make.

Most of these drawbacks are not unique to the government; they are shared by many large organizations. And perhaps they all amount to saying nothing more than that people who enjoy the risks and rewards of self-employment will find less satisfaction working for the government. They are worth considering, however, before you decide to build a government career.

## THE MAJOR REWARD

The economic benefits of government employment may or may not outweigh the drawbacks. For millions of government employees, however, the equation is not between the money you get and the hassles you go through. The reward isn't in the paycheck; it's in the people you help. These jobs are sometimes referred to as public service. The rewards of public service are in the good that is accomplished, the ignorance that is corrected, the sickness that is healed, and the fears that are assuaged. The major benefits of government employment are intangible—most importantly, the opportunity to serve the public good and have a direct impact on other people. As a government official, social worker, teacher, police officer, or firefighter, you will be able to see how your work benefits individuals and the community at large.

## CHAPTER 4

# HIRING PROCEDURES

The first step in seeking a particular government job is to learn what hiring procedures are used to fill it. For some jobs, you must be elected. For others, you are appointed by an elected official who has a free hand in making the appointment, subject to review by the board or legislature. These jobs are usually for a limited term; often, you lose your job if the person who appointed you is not reelected. These elected and appointed positions are the stuff of local politics. In general, a person who decides on policies is likely to hold one of them.

Most government workers are neither elected nor appointed in this way, however. They are appointed, or hired, according to some kind of merit or civil service system. Usually, they keep their jobs without regard to political events. People who put government policy into action are likely to be hired in accordance with a merit system.

For any given occupation, most governments use similar procedures. Mayors and sheriffs, for example, are almost always elected. City managers and police chiefs are appointed. Police officers must qualify by a series of tests. Teachers are selected by educational standards. Of course, one government will sometimes follow a different procedure for a particular occupation. And some jobs in one occupation might be handled differently than most.

The job of secretary is usually a merit position, but the mayor's secretary, or administrative assistant, is likely to be appointed.

## FEDERAL HIRING PROCESSES

At one time, the standard way to apply for a federal government job was to complete and submit the SF-171 Application for Federal Employment, and in some cases supplemental or related application forms. However, these forms became obsolete in the mid-1990s. If you see a reference to such forms, it is no longer valid.

Today, applicants for federal employment may apply in any of the following ways: submit a resume, complete and submit the Optional Application for Federal Employment (form OF-612), or submit an application in another written format of choice.

In some cases, especially when electronic application processing systems are used or when jobs require special skills, it may be necessary to complete other specialized application forms.

## MERIT SYSTEMS

Merit systems are used by all the states and most large city and county governments for at least some positions. The larger a government is, the more likely it is to have a merit system, which is why the majority of government jobs are covered by such systems even though only a bare majority of governments use them.

Under a merit system, the duties of people in a given job are clearly defined, and the qualifications required of someone who can hold that job are also spelled out in detail. All applicants for a position must be ranked according to their skills and training; the position must then be offered to one of the most highly ranked applicants.

Note that the job need not go to the highest-ranked individual, just one of the highest ranked. The person doing the hiring, therefore, has some leeway in reaching a final decision. A school principal, for example, often has the last word with regard to a new teacher, and a program manager can usually hire any one of several qualified applicants. This leeway is why you must actively hunt for a government job, and not just wait for your name to come to the top of a list. People are more likely to hire someone who has contacted them than someone who is only a name on a piece of paper.

The nuts and bolts of a merit system differ from one government to another. But in all of them, when an agency—be it a school, a police department, or a hospital—needs to hire someone, it usually issues an announcement of some kind indicating that workers are sought in one occupation or another.

## REAL WORLD HIRING CONSIDERATIONS

In an ideal world, all applicants for employment in either the private or public sector would be treated equally and judged solely on the basis of test performance and a well-structured interview. We all know, however, that in the real world vacancies in the private sector are often filled using such criteria as family or friend recommendation, networking, political connections, and so on.

The public sector is not free from the same influences. While eventually the applicant must satisfactorily complete the more formal application requirements for a job, other factors will affect who gets the position. And this is not all to the bad. The person doing the hiring is, above all, interested in filling the vacancy with someone of good character, with satisfactory work habits, and with a stable lifestyle who will fit in well with the other people in the workplace. If that hirer consistently chooses people who leave after a short time, miss a number of workdays, or cause trouble with other employees, he or she will soon lose the authority to hire. He or she may also lose opportunities for career advancement on the grounds of poor judgment—or worse.

In his excellent book *The Complete Guide to Public Employment,* Dr. Ronald L. Krannich suggested that as many as 70 percent of high-level government vacancies may be somewhat less than fully open and competitive. He termed the widespread use of an unfair tactic in filling vacancies "wiring." This is a system of informally preselecting candidates and then writing a job description that is guaranteed to make them the best qualified for the job. He suggested that the practice may be unethical or unfair, but it is not illegal. It is, he said, "...business as usual. And it takes place in most units of government to some degree." Entry-level jobs are less likely to be affected by such practices, but even at that level you will want to do your best to make yourself more than just another properly filled out application form. A sincere recommendation from a friend already employed by a unit of state or local government will always be of benefit to you. Just be sure that your formal application will back up the informal help you get.

## TYPES OF JOB ANNOUNCEMENTS

Announcements can be a single page or a small booklet. Announcements almost always indicate the occupations being filled, their salary range, the qualifications required, the duties performed in the job, application procedures, and sources of more information.

Three different types of announcements are common.

- *Open announcement.* This means that applications are always accepted. Typically, this procedure is followed only for occupations with steady turnover, especially in the clerical field.
- *Announcement of an examination.* This means that applications are being accepted for evaluation or for a test; only after

the evaluation will people be considered for actual job openings as they arise.

- *Position announcement.* This means that applications are being accepted for a job that is currently available. In many cases, the people doing the hiring only consider applicants who have already been evaluated as a result of an announcement of an examination.

Note that you must often answer two announcements to find one job: First, an announcement of an examination, and second, a position announcement. This means that *you cannot look for a job on Friday and start work on Monday.* Even for clerical positions, where the need is constant and the evaluation process streamlined, you can easily spend from three to six months between the day you decide to look for a job and the day you start work. In many other occupations—such as police officer, firefighter, and teacher—hiring normally takes place only once a year. If you miss the date on which applications to take a test are being accepted, you may have to wait an entire year before you can apply. The test itself may be some months later than the cut-off date for applications, and actual hiring may not take place for several months more. As a consequence, *three years* can pass between your decision to seek a job and your first paycheck. If you do miss the filing date, you'll at least have plenty of time to prepare for the test.

## GENERAL REQUIREMENTS AND TESTS

Besides the specific qualifications for the job, applicants must usually meet some general requirements. United States citizenship is often required. Many state and local governments also prefer to hire residents as much as possible, but as a practical matter, they will hire otherwise qualified people for hard-to-fill jobs. According to

John Zehrig in *Careers in State and Local Government,* only about half of all governments require residency.

Governments often—but not always—have a standard procedure to evaluate job applicants. The procedure is often called an examination, although no test might be given. The most frequently used evaluation procedures are the following:

- *Written tests.* Often multiple choice, samples of the tests are usually available from the government. Commercial publishers also sell books of sample tests for many occupations.
- *Performance tests.* Applicants for clerical and craft jobs must often show that they can operate the equipment or use the tools needed on the job.
- *Physical agility.* Applicants for police, firefighter, sanitation, or other positions that require specific levels of strength or agility must take tests designed to show that they can perform the same type of tasks as workers in the occupation.
- *Medical examinations.* Generally, applicants should be in good health. For some jobs, such as firefighter and police officer, standards are more rigorous than usual.
- *Ratings of education, training, and experience.* For many jobs, especially at the professional entry level, candidates are judged on the basis of the appropriateness of their education and experience to the occupation. An announcement that a government is accepting applications for such an evaluation should indicate the kind of education and experience sought. If you fill out such an application, it is your responsibility to make sure that your forms have all the needed information, even to the point of using the very words of the job description where appropriate. *Your rating depends exclusively on the evaluator's ability to find the required qualifications on your application.*
- *Interviews.* These are similar to the rating of education and experience described above. Interviews are used for occupa-

tions in which workers have frequent contact with the public, including police officer, firefighter, and claims examiner.

- *All of the above.* For some jobs—police recruits and fire-fighter recruits, for example—all these evaluation procedures are used.

In addition, many employers, both private and public, require job applicants to sign affidavits that attest to the applicants' marital status, citizenship, and criminal record, if any. It is a mistake to attempt to conceal any facts about yourself through failing to be truthful. You will spend a lot of time and money and suffer the loss of your hopes and dreams if you are found out. If you lie, the chances are excellent that you *will* be found out. And, your signature on a false affidavit is all the grounds needed to terminate your employment. You will be better off if you are truthful, even if you must ask permission to explain the circumstances behind some of your responses. An arrest, long in the past, followed by years of good citizenship, may not be a problem. An alcohol problem followed by years of sobriety should not stigmatize you. Most people are fair-minded about mistakes from which others learned. If they are not, better to know that up front and not six months or two years into a job you enjoy and don't want to lose.

In most cases, after you take a test or submit evidence of your education and experience, the personnel department rates you and notifies you of your rating. If you score highly enough, you are eligible for employment. Even a high rating is no guarantee of a job, however, and—as said above—your chances of employment are almost always improved if you go out and look for a position rather than wait for the personnel department to send your name to someone with a vacancy.

## CHAPTER 5

# SUCCEEDING IN JOB SEARCHES

When you envision this part of your job search, you might see a hurdle to leap over, or a hoop to jump through, or a barrier to knock down. That is how many people think of resumes, application forms, cover letters, tests, and interviews. But you do not have to think of them that way. They are not ways to keep you from a job; they are ways for you to show an employer how good you really are. After all, you are going to get a job. It is just a question of which one.

Governments, like other employers, want to hire people who can do the job. To learn who these people are, they use resumes, application forms, written tests, performance tests, medical examinations, and interviews. This chapter points out ways you can use all these different evaluation procedures to best advantage.

## DEVELOPING EFFECTIVE RESUMES
## AND APPLICATION FORMS

Resumes and application forms are two ways to achieve the same goal: to give the employer written evidence of your qualifications. When creating a resume, you need two different kinds of information: facts about yourself and facts about the job you want. You then present the facts about yourself in terms of the job. You have more freedom with a resume—you can put your best points first and avoid blanks. But even on application forms, you can describe your qualifications in terms of the job's duties.

## WORK SHEETS

The best way to save your own time, and that of others, is to put together a work sheet that contains all the information you will need to draw up a basic resume—one that can be adapted for use in a variety of situations. Your work sheet should also include any information that you might need when you have to fill out an application at the job site. You can guess the impression that is made by applicants who can't find their social security numbers or the addresses of former employers. Here are some things your work sheet should cover, but you will probably want to add others:

- Your current address and phone number. If you are hard to track down during business hours, also supply another number of someone reliable who will agree to take phone messages for you. You may also want to put down your last couple of addresses, particularly if you haven't been at your current address for a fairly long time. Include an E-mail address, if you have one.
- Your career goals, carefully thought out and edited to a concise paragraph. In a resume, you can wax a bit eloquent, but job application forms rarely give you much room for answers.
- Social Security number.
- Experience (paid and volunteer)—complete with dates of employment, name and full address of employer, job title, starting and finishing salaries. You also will need to give your reason for leaving, and there are several that are acceptable— moving, returning to school, seeking a better position. If the circumstances of your leaving a job are unhappy, you may

omit giving them, but be prepared to answer truthfully, if asked. You may have been fired, but if that was because you refused to perform foolishly dangerous tasks, for example, it could even be a plus for you.

- Education—the last school you attended, its correct address, the years you attended, the diploma or degree you earned, and your major course of study.
- Other qualifications—special skills, hobbies, organizations you belong to, honors you have received. These activities often tell more about you as a person than do your work-for-pay activities.
- Office equipment, tools, machines you have used successfully. Computer skills can be especially important.
- List of references. You will want four or five business and personal references. Be sure to get their permission to be approached. Supply correctly spelled names, current addresses, and telephone numbers. Indicate which are personal and which are business references.
- Some books will advise that you come right out and say the salary you expect to be paid. You may want to give a range that you find acceptable, or you may want to leave the matter open. Opportunities for advancement, geographic location, and opportunities for travel may be of greater importance to you than a few dollars difference in salary at the beginning of your career. You don't want to limit your choices arbitrarily.
- Be frank about any disabilities you may have. Federal law protects your rights as a disabled person. Better you acknowledge your disability and then stress your *abilities* right from the start.
- If you have ever been convicted of a crime—admit it. You need not say anything about any charge of which you were acquitted.
- Finally, make several photocopies of your work sheet. If you fold it and carry it around to many places, it will soon become

dog-eared and make it appear that you have been looking for work for several decades. Put one copy in a very safe place. After going through all of the hours it took to assemble your information, you don't want to have to start over!

Next, gather specific information about the jobs you are applying for. You need to know the pay range, the education and experience usually required, hours and shifts usually worked. Most important, you need to know the job duties (so that you can describe your experience in terms of those duties). Study the job description; a government announcement might even have a checklist that assigns a numerical weight to different qualifications so that you can be certain as to which is the most important. If the announcement or ad is vague, call the agency to learn what is sought.

Once you have the information needed, you can prepare a resume. You may need to prepare more than one master resume if you are going to look for different kinds of jobs.

The way you arrange your resume depends on how well your experience seems to prepare you for the position you want. Basically, you can describe your most recent job first and work backwards (chronological resume); or group similar skills together (functional resume); or you can combine the two forms—as in the example provided. No matter which form you use, the following advice generally applies:

- *Use specifics.* A vague description of your duties will make only a vague impression.
- *Identify accomplishments.* If you improved productivity, reduced costs, increased membership, or achieved some other goal, say so.
- *Prepare your resume with a computer and good-quality printer using a standard font.* (Printed resumes are becoming more common, but employers do not indicate a preference for the use of fancy typefaces and design.)

- *Keep the length down to two pages at the most.* (The sample in this chapter is a single page in its original format.)
- *Remember your mother's advice not to say anything if you can't say something nice.* Leave *all* embarrassing or negative information off the resume (but be ready to deal with it in a positive fashion at the interview).
- *Proofread the master copy carefully.*
- *Have someone else proofread the master copy carefully.*
- *Have a third person proofread the master copy carefully.*
- Use the best quality photocopying machine or printer and good white or off-white paper.

Many government agencies make more use of *application forms* than of resumes. The forms suit the style of large organizations because people can find information more quickly if it always appears in the same place. No matter how rigid the form appears to be, you can still use it to show why you are the person for the job being filled.

At first glance, application forms seem to give a job hunter no leeway. The forms certainly do not have the flexibility that a resume does, but you can use them to your best advantage. Remember that the attitude of the person reading the form is not "Let's find out why this person is unqualified," but "Maybe this is the person we want." Use all the parts of the form—experience blocks, education blocks, and others—to show that *the person is you.*

Here's some general advice on application forms:

- Request two copies of the form. If only one is provided, photocopy it before you make a mark on it. You'll need more than one copy to prepare rough drafts.
- Read the whole form before you start completing it.
- Prepare a master copy if the same form is used by several agencies. Do not fill in the specific job applied for, date, and

**SAMPLE RESUME**

---

Tracy P. Ramirez

Address | Telephone Number
123 New Street | 815-555-9248
Anytown, CA 90210 | (Another number,
  |   if needed)
  | E-mail if applicable

Position sought: xxxxxxxxxxxxxxxxxxxxxxxxxxxxxx
xxxxxxxxxxxxxxxxxxxxxxxxxxxxxxxxxxxxxxxxxxxxxx
xxxxxxxxxxxxxxxxxxxxxxxxxxxxxxxxxxxxxxxxxx.

**EDUCATION**
School, address, diploma or degree, year of completion.

**COURSES RELEVANT TO POSITION**
List those courses that add to your desirability as a future employee.

**WORK EXPERIENCE**
Start with your most recent employment experience and tell specifically what your duties were and what you accomplished in the situation. List both full- and part-time jobs.

**VOLUNTEER OR EXTRACURRICULAR EXPERIENCE**
*Be specific* about what you did with organizations—offices held, honors awarded.

**REFERENCES**
List one or two business and personal references. Be prepared to supply more, if required.

signature on the master form. Fill in that information on the photocopies as you submit them.

- Type your entries on the application form if possible. If the form has lots of little lines that are hard to type within, ask if you can prepare a word processed version on a piece of blank paper that will fit in the space, paste the paper over the form, and photocopy the finished product. Such a procedure results in a much neater, easier-to-read page. Or see if on-line application options are available.

- Leave no blanks; enter *n/a* (for "not applicable") when the information requested does not apply to you; this tells people checking the form that you did not simply skip the question.

- Carry a resume and a copy of other frequently asked-for information (such as previous addresses) with you when visiting potential employers in case you must fill out an application on the spot. Whenever possible, however, fill the form out at home and mail it in with a resume and a cover letter that highlight your strong points.

## WRITING INTRIGUING COVER LETTERS

You will need a cover letter whenever you send a resume or application form to a potential employer. The letter should capture the employer's attention, show why you are writing, indicate why your employment will benefit the company, and ask for an interview.

*Each letter should be addressed by name to the person you want to talk with.* That person is the one who can hire you. This is almost certainly not someone in the personnel department, and it is probably not a department head either. It is most likely to be the person who will actually supervise you once you start work. Call the company to make sure you have the right name. And spell it correctly.

*The opening should appeal to the reader.* Cover letters are sales letters. Sales are made after you capture the person's attention. You capture someone's attention most easily by talking about them rather than yourself. Throughout this book, periodicals and associations that publish periodicals are listed. These periodicals can give you information you need to make the kind of personal tie-in that you are looking for, such as a special project that is underway. Other ways to catch the reader's eye besides mentioning projects under development are references to awards a person has recently received and favorable comments about the program that the person has run. If you are answering an ad, you can mention it. If someone that you know suggested that you write, use that person's name (with permission, of course).

*The body of the letter gives a brief description of your qualifications,* and refers to the resume, where your sales campaign can continue.

*You cannot have what you do not ask for.* Ask for an interview. Suggest a time. State that you will confirm the appointment.

*Use a standard complementary close and signature block.* Include a phone number—which is not yet part of a standard signature block, although it is found on most letterheads. An E-mail address may also be included.

In order to be specific and relevant, each letter must be written individually. Each letter must also be typed perfectly. Word processing equipment can help. Frequently, only the address, first paragraph, and specifics concerning an interview will vary. These items are easily changed with word processing software.

## SAMPLE COVER LETTER

123 New Street
Anytown, CA 90210
January 24, 2001

Ms. Jane Christopher
Executive Director
Warren-Sharpe Community Center
472 South 21st Avenue
Allen, CA 90052

Dear Ms. Christopher,

Your announcement of a job opening at the Warren-Sharpe Community Center is of great interest to me.

I have six years of experience, both as a volunteer and as a part-time student worker, in programs similar to yours. In addition, I am fluent in the Spanish language, and would, from the start, be able to communicate easily with the population you serve.

In addition, my college training has prepared me for a career in community social services. I have taken courses in sociology, psychology, social work, and recreational activities.

In my volunteer and part-time jobs I have worked with infants, assisting at a day-care center; coached track and volleyball; and acted as an ombudsman at a senior citizen housing center.

I believe I could bring the training and experience you are looking for to the job and am available for an interview at your convenience. My resume is enclosed, and I look forward to hearing from you.

Sincerely,

Tracy P. Ramirez
815-555-9248

## PERFORMING WELL ON TESTS

A man with a violin case stood on a subway platform in the Bronx. He asked a conductor, "How do you get to Carnegie Hall?" The conductor replied, "Practice! Practice! Practice!"

That old joke holds good advice for test takers (and people preparing for interviews). The tests given to job applicants fall into four categories: general aptitude tests, practical tests, tests of physical agility, and medical examinations. You can practice for the first three. If the fourth is required, learn as soon as possible what the disqualifying conditions are, then have your physician examine you for them so that you do not spend years training for a job that you will not be allowed to hold.

To practice for a test, you must learn what the test is. That means you must know what job you want to apply for and what government you want to work for. You then contact each government and learn what tests are given. Often the government will provide a sample of the test. For a physical agility test or practical test, it should explain exactly what you will have to do. For written tests, governments often issue a booklet; it may only give you an idea of the kinds of questions asked, however. Some commercial publishers sell books with many complete tests in them.

Ask for such books at your library and also contact workers in the occupation and ask them about the tests they took.

If you practice beforehand, you'll be better prepared and less nervous on the day of the test. That will put you ahead of the competition. You can also improve your performance by following this advice:

- Make a list of what you will need at the test center; check it before leaving the house.
- Get a good night's sleep.
- Be at the test center early—at least fifteen minutes early.

- Read the instructions carefully; make sure they do not differ from the samples you practiced with.
- Generally, speed counts; do not linger over difficult questions.
- Learn whether guessing is penalized. Most tests are scored by counting up the right answers; guessing is all to the good. Some tests are scored by counting the right answers and deducting partial credit for wrong answers; blind guessing will lose you points—but if you can eliminate two wrong choices in multiple choice tests, a guess might still pay off.

### WINNING AT INTERVIEWS

For many of us, interviews are the most fearsome part of finding a job. But they are also our best chance to show an employer our best side. Interviews are far more flexible than application forms or tests. Use that flexibility to your advantage. As with tests, you can reduce your anxiety and improve your performance by preparing for your interviews ahead of time.

You can begin by considering what interviewers want to know. You represent a risk to the agency. A hiring mistake is expensive in terms of lost productivity, wasted training money, and the cost of finding a replacement. To lessen the risk, interviewers try to select people who are highly motivated, understand what the job entails, and show that they can perform it.

You show that you are highly motivated by learning about the agency before the interview, by dressing appropriately, and by being well mannered—which means that you greet the interviewer by name, you do not chew gum, you do not smoke, you listen attentively, and you thank the interviewer at the end of the session. You also show motivation by expressing interest in the job at the end of the interview.

You show an understanding of what the job entails and that you can perform it when you explain how your qualifications prepare you for specific duties as described in the announcement and when you ask intelligent questions about the nature of the work and the training provided to new workers.

One of the best ways to prepare for an interview is to have some practice sessions with a friend or two. Here is a list of some commonly asked questions to get you started.

- Why did you apply for this job?
- What do you know about this job or agency?
- Why did you choose this career?
- Why should I hire you?
- What would you do if...(usually filled in with a work-related crisis)
- How would you describe yourself?
- What would you like to tell me about yourself?
- What are your major strengths?
- What are your major weaknesses?
- What type of work do you like to do best?

Your strategy should be to concentrate on the job and your ability to do it no matter what the question seems to be asking. If asked for a strength, mention something job-related. If asked for a weakness, mention a job-related strength (you work too hard, you worry too much about details, you always have to see the big picture). If asked about a disability or a specific negative factor in your past—a criminal record, a failure in school, being fired—be prepared to stress what you learned from the experience, how you have overcome the shortcoming, and how you are now in a position to do a better job. Salary negotiation is a special subject in itself. Avoid discussing salaries and fringe benefits until you have a job offer.

So far, only the interviewer's questions have been discussed. But an interview will be a two-way conversation. You really do need to learn more about the position to find out if you want the job. Given how frustrating it is to look for a job, you do not want to take just any position only to learn after two weeks that you can't stand the place and have to look for another job right away. Here are some questions for you to ask the interviewer.

- What would a day on this job be like?
- Whom would I report to? May I meet this person?
- Whom would I supervise? May I meet them?
- How important is this job to the agency?
- What training programs are offered?
- What advancement opportunities are available?
- Why did the last person leave this job?
- What is that person doing now?
- What is the greatest challenge of this position?

After you ask such questions, listen carefully to the interviewer's answer, then, if at all possible, point to something about yourself that fits with the answer. You might notice that questions about salary and fringe benefits are not included in the above list. Your focus at a first interview should be the agency and what you can do for it, not what the agency can pay you. The salary range will be given in the position announcement and information on the usual fringe benefits will be available from the personnel department. Once you have been offered a position, you can negotiate about the salary.

At the end of the interview, be sure you know what the next step will be: whether you should contact the agency again, whether you should provide more information, whether more interviews must be conducted, and when a final decision should be reached. End on a positive note by reaffirming your interest in the position and pointing out why you will be a good choice. Finally, thank the interviewer.

Immediately after the interview, make notes of what went well and what you would like to improve on next time. To show your interest in the position, send a follow-up letter to the interviewer, providing further information on some point raised in the interview and thanking the interviewer once again.

## CHAPTER 6

# LOCATING JOBS

If you seek a job in a merit system, this chapter is for you. If you want to learn more about elected positions, see the chapter "Running for Office."

## WHERE TO START

The federal government, every state, most cities, and many counties have agencies that provide information about how jobs are filled. You can learn the names of others from government directories, which can be found in the public library. Besides directories and job announcements, the library will have many other books and some magazines that give advice on finding work. The government section of telephone books also indicates whom to contact for job information, in many cases.

Professional organizations and unions are among the nongovernment groups that often have information for job seekers. No matter which occupations interest you, some association of people who work in it probably exists, and you can find these listed under *Associations* in the yellow pages of the phone book. Your library probably also has a directory of associations. Some associations publish explicit career information, but even those that do not often have useful material such as a periodical that contains articles on salaries and working conditions or help-wanted ads and position announcements. Even the association's membership directory is helpful because it will name people with whom you can discuss the occupation. These materials are often available on request from the association.

## FINDING ANNOUNCEMENTS

The sources of information given above are useful for both general leads and specific help. But once you decide on an occupation and a government career, specific information is what you need.

In order to land a government job, you usually have to find an announcement, the different kinds of which are described in the previous chapter. First you need an announcement that a test is being given or that people's qualifications for an occupation are being evaluated. You need to find *position* or *job vacancy announcements* so that you can apply for a job, since no matter how highly you are rated by a personnel department, you usually have to discover your own opening. An evaluation isn't a guarantee; it's a fishing license. And be sure to start looking long before you'll need a job, since landing a job can easily take more than a year.

Governments publicize their announcements several ways. The following are the most common:

- *Bulletin boards* in government buildings are almost always used. The obvious place is near the personnel office, but announcements are also found in courthouses, hospitals, and other locations.
- *Websites* include sections on job openings or employment.
- *Public libraries,* perhaps because branches are often located throughout a government's area, often receive copies of all announcements.

- *Local newspapers* print brief notices of job openings in the help-wanted section.
- *Job banks,* which are run by Job Service or related state offices, usually list both state and local position announcements as well as other jobs. The locations of Job Service offices are given in the state government section of telephone books. The Job Bank, or listing, is also sometimes available at libraries and schools.
- *Community organizations,* such as the YMCA, NAACP, and churches, receive announcements; Baltimore sends such notices to more than one hundred organizations.
- *College placement offices* often post job announcements; you can usually check the bulletin board even if you are not enrolled.
- *Newspapers and other periodicals* aimed at government workers—federal, state, or local—carry position announcements. An example is the *Federal Times,* an independent weekly targeted to federal employees. Besides the announcements, the articles in such newspapers can point you toward agencies that are likely to begin hiring even before an official announcement is issued.
- *Publications of associations of government workers* carry both job notices and pertinent articles on trends. Titles of such publications appear throughout this book.
- *Publications of associations in fields with many government workers,* such as civil engineering and nursing, also carry both help-wanted ads and informative articles. These publications, too, are listed elsewhere in this book.
- *Commercial publications* also collect and print the job vacancy announcements for several agencies or governments; some such publications are limited to a single level of government, such as federal, state, city, or county; others focus on all governments within a region. Titles of some of these publica-

tions are given in Appendix A. Check with a librarian to learn which would be most useful to you.

- *Recorded telephone messages.* Many governments, especially the larger ones, have regularly updated recorded messages concerning openings and announcements. The number will usually be listed in the government section of the telephone book under the agency's name.

When you find an announcement, make careful note of the following information:

- The date by which you must apply.
- If the announcement is for an examination, the titles of the occupations covered.
- If the announcement is for positions, the titles of the jobs and where they are located.
- The minimum education and experience required.
- The job duties.
- Where to send your application.
- Whom to contact for more information, if stated.

If you are going to be evaluated on the basis of your education and experience rather than by a test, the announcement's description of the job's duties can help you use the terms the personnel office will recognize when you write about your qualifications.

## USING OTHER EMPLOYMENT RESOURCES

Finding announcements should not be the only focus of your job search, however. Many jobs are filled without such a notice being made; in other cases, the notice is put up only after a preferred job candidate has been found. Therefore, in addition to looking for announcements, you should look for potential employers in other ways.

Begin with relatives and friends who either work for the government or have the kind of occupation you want in the private sector. Government is so large that you or a member of your family is bound to know someone with a government job. Such a person can start you on the track of finding the right people to contact. One contact will lead to another, and you might eventually find someone who is just getting ready to hire a new worker. Even if the contacts don't point you toward a job, they can frequently offer valuable advice on filling out applications and on the current job market.

You should also contact the agencies that you know employ people who do the kind of work you want. You can then write, telephone, or visit the agency.

Private employment agencies listed under employment services in the yellow pages may also have information about government jobs. If you use such an agency, make sure you know if you are going to have to pay any fees, and if so, how much. In most cases, the person who hires you will pay the fee, not you. In others, you will pay the fee. Most agencies are reputable and will give you fair service for your money; but some are not. If you do have to pay, you should grill the agency to learn exactly what it can do for you before you make any final decision or sign any papers. Ask for the names of other clients and contact them to learn if they thought the agency's fees were worth paying; contact their supervisors, too, to learn if they use the agency very often. You can also check with the Better Business Bureau to ask whether or not the private employment agency has a good business history.

Lastly, you can go back to the beginning of this chapter. The sources of general information given there can also point you toward contacts with hiring officials in the government.

## CHAPTER 7

# RUNNING FOR OFFICE

A great many officeholders in federal, state and local government are elected. Exactly which officials are elected varies a great deal, but among them may be the following:

*Federal:*
U.S. Senator
Member, House of Representatives
Vice President
President

*State:*
Legislator, delegate, representative, senator, or assemblyman
Governor
Lieutenant governor
Attorney general
Treasurer
Secretary of state
Auditor
Superintendent of education or public instruction
Member of board of education
Commissioner of agriculture
Commissioner of public utilities
Controller
Insurance commissioner

Commissioner of public lands
Commissioner of labor
Commissioner of mines
Judge

*Local:*

Member of the board of supervisors, city council, town council,
    or board of commissioners
Mayor
Assessor
Auditor
Clerk—town, county, or court
Coroner
District attorney or county prosecutor
Health officer
Public defender
Public administrator
Recorder
Sheriff
Superintendent of schools
Member of the board of education
Surveyor
Tax collector
Treasurer
Judge

The decision to seek one of these jobs should not be taken
lightly. But these are the jobs where real change is possible.

## DECIDING TO RUN

Like any major choice, the decision to run for office can be broken into smaller components. Here are some questions to consider.

*Do you have the time to mount a campaign?*
- Will your job suffer?
- Will family responsibilities suffer?
- Do you have the support to mount a campaign?
- Will your family approve?
- Will your family help?
- Will regular party members help?
- Are you known in the community?
- Will civic organizations or their members support you?

*Do you have the financial resources for the campaign?*
- How much money will be needed? (For some major offices, multimillion dollar campaigns are common.)
- What finance laws govern the election? *The Book of States* has this information for state offices.
- Will individuals and groups that support you back that commitment with money?

*Do you meet the requirements for the job?*
- What are the age and residency requirements?
- Is a particular occupational certification, such as a law degree, required?
- Can you meet the filing dates?
- Must you submit a citizen's petition?
- What is the filing fee?

*Are you qualified for the job?*
- Is special knowledge needed?
- Do you have positions on the issues?

*Will the voters recognize that you have the qualifications?*
- Are you known to them?
- Are your positions close enough to theirs so that you can make a case?

*Can you afford to win?*

*Do you deserve the job?*
- Are you the best person for the position? Why?
- How will the community benefit from your winning?

*Do you really want the job?*

Remember that some of these jobs are very time-consuming and pay very little. You must ask if you can live on the salary, if you can afford the time away from your regular career, and if you can afford the time away from your family. In other words, will the benefits balance the commitment in time and energy required?

Incidentally, if you plan a career in politics, pay particular attention to the questions on support. You can build support for a future race by being active in community organizations, building a network of potential supporters, and working in campaigns for other people. Agreement seems universal that the best way to prepare for a campaign is to work in someone else's.

## BUILDING A STAFF AND RAISING MONEY

To win an election, all you need do is receive more votes than your opponents. Contacting and convincing voters, therefore, is the obvious path to victory. Doing so requires a combination of people and money; one leads to the other, though neither guarantees victory. Supporters give money; money allows you to build the organization to recruit more supporters.

The basic group of supporters is the campaign committee. Typically, it would have at least the following members:

- Campaign manager (in most cases, the more experienced, the better; nonrunning current and former officeholders can recommend people)

- Treasurer (who must be thoroughly familiar with the finance and financial disclosure laws)
- Campaign chairperson (to organize all the other workers)
- Publicity chairperson

Naturally, in a larger campaign, the committee might be larger. Publicity, for example, can be split into special events, advertising, and canvassing.

The campaign staff augments the committee. The nucleus of a staff should suggest itself from the questions on support when you decided to run—family, friends, people you know in community organizations. You will also want to recruit many people you do not yet know, of course. Sources of volunteers include the membership lists of organizations, the young Democrats or young Republicans, people who worked in previous campaigns, college campuses, senior centers, and members of political action committees (all PAC's are registered with the Federal Election Commission). Once a start has been made, the staff itself will be a major source of additional volunteers.

Raising money causes more anxiety for many people than building a staff. For example, when asked, "What do you find most difficult about campaigning?" a recent senatorial candidate replied, "Raising money... It's the universal complaint of people in politics." However, some people love to do fund-raising. And the millions on millions of dollars raised by candidates each year show that many people will contribute to campaigns.

The sources of financial help are pretty much the same as the sources of volunteers. Again, you begin with family and friends, members of organizations that support you, and the contributors to previous campaigns.

## LEARNING FROM OTHERS

Needless to say, far more advice is available on campaigning for office than can be given here. Experienced campaigners can provide useful information on using the media, defining the issues, canvassing techniques, money-raising techniques, polling the electorate, using voter roles, determining the amount of money needed, determining the minimum staff requirements, budgeting the cash flow of the campaign, budgeting volunteers' time, planning the candidate's schedule, and many other subjects.

The following organizations are sources of that information:

Democratic National Committee
    430 S. Capitol Street SE
    Washington, DC 20003

National Women's Political Caucus
    1630 Connecticut Avenue NW
    #201
    Washington, DC 20009

Republican National Committee
    310 First Street SE
    Washington, DC 20003

For information on regulations governing candidates and elections, contact the board of elections, clerk's office, or secretary of state's office. Information on federal regulations is available from the Federal Election Commission, 999 E Street NW, Washington, DC 20463.

Besides the above organizations, a number of books have been written that are filled with nuts-and-bolts information. A few have a very specific ideological bent; that does not make their advice less useful, however. Several of these books are listed in Appendix A.

## CHAPTER 8

# JOBS THROUGHOUT THE GOVERNMENT

Most government occupations are concentrated in one agency or another. Some occupations, however, are found in all sorts of different agencies. The largest of these occupations are discussed in this chapter.

## PROFESSIONAL OCCUPATIONS

Among the professional occupations spread through many federal, state, and local government agencies are accountant, lawyer, computer programmer and computer systems analyst, office manager, purchasing agent, and personnel officer. These jobs usually require at least a college diploma in a field related to the occupation, although technical and clerical employees are sometimes promoted into a few of them.

## ACCOUNTANTS

Governments make no profits and pay no taxes, but government accountants still have plenty to do. Accountants keep track of an organization's assets and liabilities. For a business, that includes figuring out if the year ended with a profit or in the red and completing complicated tax forms. For a government, it includes preparing budgets, keeping track of incoming money (both taxes and transfers from higher governments) and payments, estimating income and expenditures for the next year or more, and analyzing the cost of doing something different ways.

Accountants use calculators and computers to organize the data they work with. They generally work in well-lit, comfortable offices for forty hours a week.

*What you should bring to this occupation.* Besides enjoying working with numbers, an accountant must have an interest in detail. In addition, accountants need communication skills to report the results of their analysis in writing and orally.

The majority of accountants have bachelor's degrees in accounting. Many accountants, however, began working as bookkeepers or accounting clerks and were promoted into accounting positions.

*The rewards.* Accountants find the orderliness of accounting procedures satisfying. If you do not like working with details and do not value order, you probably will not enjoy accounting.

The average salary for 1998 was $37,860, according to the Bureau of Labor Statistics.

*Where to find a job.* A wide range of government agencies employ accountants. In 1999, accountants employed by the federal government had average salaries of approximately $58,200 yearly. Starting annual salaries ranged from about $20,000 to $31,200 in 1999.

Budget agencies, controllers' offices, tax assessors' offices, treasury departments, and other agencies that are responsible for financial matters or auditing services have a higher-than-average proportion of these workers. The employment of accountants throughout the economy is projected to increase faster than the average during the next decade.

*Where to learn more.* Several associations provide information about accounting, including the following:

American Institute of Certified Public Accountants
201 Plaza III
Jersey City, NJ 07311

Institute of Management Accountants
10 Paragon Drive
Montvale, NJ 07645

## CLERICAL OCCUPATIONS

The largest number of occupations found throughout the government is in the clerical group. Administrative assistants, keyboarders, and word processors alone number almost a million. Other large or important clerical occupations are accounting clerk and bookkeeper, clerical supervisor, file clerk, and town/county clerk. Besides being large, the first three of these occupations have high turnover. This combination means that openings are numerous.

High school graduation is usually the minimum qualification; you can find a job much more easily if you can key at least forty words per minute. Bookkeeper and accounting clerk jobs may require high school or even junior college courses in business math, bookkeeping, and accounting principles.

## WORD PROCESSORS AND
## ADMINISTRATIVE ASSISTANTS

In some other world, offices might be able to do without administrative assistants and word processors, but not in this one. Word processors prepare material primarily from manuscripts or recorded dictation. Administrative assistants have many additional duties, including running and maintaining the photocopy machine, organizing files, providing information to callers and visitors, scheduling appointments, and making travel arrangements. Word processors use the latest office equipment to process information and data and to keep records. They are also responsible for editing and storing and revising these materials. Word processors also may be required to function as keyboarders, answer telephones, and operate other office machines. They also need to have good spelling, grammar, and punctuation skills.

Word processing positions are frequently entry-level jobs in the workplace, but they can lead to higher paying jobs later on. They may become supervisors of their department, administrative assistants, statistical clerks, or stenographers.

Most administrative assistants, keyboarders, and word processors work in comfortable, well-lit—but sometimes noisy and hectic—offices for forty hours a week.

*What you should bring to this occupation.* Successful administrative assistants are able to handle many things at once, organize their own work, and get along with others. Increasingly, they must be adaptable because of the rapid introduction of new word processing and computing equipment. Each new machine means a change in how to do things, and new machines seem to come along just when the last one has been mastered.

Administrative assistants and keyboarders, too, should be good spellers and know the essentials of English punctuation and grammar. They also need some mechanical skills to maintain and perform minor repairs to the equipment they use.

Few employers hire anyone who cannot key at least forty words per minute. Higher speeds are preferred. A high school education is usually required.

*The rewards.* These workers receive satisfaction from contributing to the success of their organizations; the more they value those goals, the more satisfied they are with their work—a point worth considering when you apply for a job.

Keyboarders and administrative assistants also are able to advance to supervisory positions; some become office managers. The chances for advancement depend in part on the way an organization is set up, and you may require additional education. Among the sources of dissatisfaction for these workers are low salaries and lack of prestige within the organization.

The average salary for word processors in 1998 was $22,590; administrative assistants earned $23,560. Salaries vary widely, however, depending on the skills and responsibilities of the worker. Administrative assistants and word processors receive the usual fringe benefits.

*Where to learn more.* General information about this occupation is available from the following association:

International Association of Administrative Professionals
   1502 NW Ambassador Drive
   P.O. Box 20404
   Kansas City, MO 64195-0404

National Association of Legal Secretaries
   2448 East Eighty-first Street
   Tulsa, OK 74137

A note on stenographers: Extensive use of recorded dictation has resulted in a decline in the employment of stenographers throughout the economy, but the decline has not been as great in state and local government. In fact, about one-third of all stenographers work for state or local governments. Many of these stenographers are court reporters who operate stenotype machines, which requires special training.

## OTHER CLERICAL OCCUPATIONS

*Bookkeepers and accounting clerks* keep track of the money that an organization takes in and pays out. They keep records in journals and ledgers or on computer disks. High school graduates usually qualify for these jobs, especially if they have learned business arithmetic, bookkeeping, and principles of accounting. The average salary for accounting clerks is in the middle third for all wage earners; the median salary in 1998 was slightly more than $23,000.

*File clerk* is an entry-level job in many large agencies. The clerk sorts letters, bills, contracts, or other documents according to the alphabet, a numerical code, or some other system and puts them where they belong. The clerk also finds and retrieves an item when it is needed. Some clerks classify the material to begin with. A high school education is usually required. The average annual salary was $16,830 in 1998.

*Town or county clerks* act as administrative assistants to the governing board, recording the minutes of meetings, answering letters, and preparing reports. They also issue and keep records of official documents, such as marriage licenses, birth certificates, and land deeds. This is usually an elected office. For more information, speak to the clerk in your area.

As the Information Age continues to develop and emerging technologies become commonplace in all offices, including state and local governments, job titles and descriptions will change also. Secretaries, for example, are now known as *administrative assistants.* The duties of the job have grown and widened until the new title more accurately reflects what anyone holding the position does in a typical day.

Because new technologies replace long-used office machines, fewer and fewer clerical opportunities now exist. There will be, however, a rapidly growing need for trained *word processors.*

Check the ads in your local paper and you will see how many employers require knowledge of the various systems now in place in even the smallest office. In larger offices there usually appears a department devoted exclusively to word processing—much like the now almost obsolete "typing pool."

This is an area of employment in which anyone who will make the effort to acquire new skills as new technology comes into the workplace will advance. Anyone trained to operate tomorrow's office machines will be a prime candidate for supervisory positions.

## CRAFT AND BLUE-COLLAR OCCUPATIONS

Several technical, service, operative, craft, and repairer occupations also have large numbers of workers in many different government agencies. These occupations include building custodian, electrician, engineering and science technician, general maintenance repairer, and guard. Some of these jobs are very routine; others are extremely varied. Some require no particular education or experience; qualifying for others takes years of training. Salaries naturally reflect these differences.

*Automotive mechanics* find out what is wrong with a car and fix it; they must be able to use tools and read shop manuals; some specialize in certain types of repairs, such as transmissions or tuneups, but most do a little bit of everything. Average wages are within the middle 40 percent for all wage earners; the median wage in 1998 was $13.16 per hour. Employment in state and local governments was about fifty thousand that year. Major employers in state and local government would be departments that own many vehicles, such as police and fire departments. Further information is available from:

Automotive Service Association
 1901 Airport Freeway
 Bedford, TX 76021

National Automotive Technicians Education Foundation
    13505 Dulles Technology Drive
    Herndon, VA 20171

*Electricians* are skilled craft workers with years of training. They install and repair the wiring in government buildings. Apprenticeship programs provide training. Electricians must be licensed. Average salaries for electricians are in the middle third for all wage earners; average weekly earnings in 1998 were $679. This is a moderate-size occupation, with a total employment of 656,000 in 1998; state and local governments employ substantial numbers. Large school systems and hospitals also employ many thousands of electricians. You can contact unions or associations such as the following:

International Brotherhood of Electrical Workers
    1125 Fifteenth Street NW
    Washington, DC 20005

*Engineering and science technicians* test equipment and use laboratory or engineering instruments. This title refers to a large group of occupations that call for similar levels of skill and training, although the specific duties vary widely. Among these occupations are drafter, electrical and electronics technician, civil engineering technician, surveyor, biological technician, sanitation technician, and pump technician. Drafting, surveying, technical, and laboratory experience or courses in technical schools or community colleges are helpful in qualifying for these jobs, but some openings are available for high school graduates. Salaries depend in part on the specific occupation. The median salary for repairers of commercial and industrial equipment was $35,588 in 1998. The median annual salary for engineering technicians in 1998 was $35,970. For more information, contact:

Accreditation Board for Engineering and Technology, Inc.
    111 Market Place, Suite 1050
    Baltimore, MD 21202

Junior Engineering Technical Society
   1420 King Street
   Alexandria, VA 22314

*Guards* patrol buildings when they are closed and keep watch over their entrances when they are open. A high school diploma is usually preferred, but not always required. In 1998, the average median salary was $16,240. Schools, hospitals, and government office buildings frequently employ guards. There are currently more than one million people employed as guards and security officers. The field is expected to grow at more than the average rate.

## CHAPTER 9

# ADMINISTRATION, LEGISLATION, AND THE COURT SYSTEM

*General control jobs* refer to *legislative, government-wide administrative,* and *judiciary functions.* Law making is the one function shared by every government. The laws are passed by city councils, county boards, state legislatures, and the U.S. Congress. They are enforced by city managers, mayors, or governors. Judges and justices of the peace determine if laws have been broken and by whom. All these occupations make up a very mixed bag. Many of those in them were either elected by the citizens or appointed by someone who was elected. They are what politics is all about.

State legislature, city councils, and county boards perform the same functions for their governments that Congress does for the federal government. They determine what the government should do and how services should be paid for. They hold hearings to consider new laws or ordinances, approve the government's budget, and either appoint or confirm the appointments of policy-making officials. Employees of the legislative branch include clerical workers, specialists such as legal analysts who can act as advisors, and lawyers. Total legislative employment is far smaller than executive employment, however.

Financial administration keeps track of the government's revenues and expenditures. Collecting taxes, preparing budgets, and monitoring expenditures are jobs done by every government. Appraising real estate is a common job at the local level.

## CITY MANAGERS

Who runs things when a committee is in charge? That's the question confronting cities and towns with a council-manager form of government. And the answer is the same for both store and city: a professional manager. Cities and towns have many different departments, each of which takes care of particular functions, such as police protection or street repair. City managers see that all the departments run smoothly.

Depending on the laws of the state and the will of the council, city managers may appoint the department heads. They usually prepare the city budget and submit it for approval. They may also suggest changes in city ordinances or policies.

City managers officially work a forty-hour week, but most will put in many more hours than that. Much of their time is spent in an office, but they may also have to travel throughout the city, attend council meetings, and so on.

*What you should bring to this occupation.* City managers usually have a master's degree in public administration, which would include such courses as municipal law, finance, and political aspects of urban problems. An internship of six to twelve months may be required. They frequently start their careers as assistants before becoming managers.

Managers are usually appointed by a council or mayor; their contracts are subject to renewal on a regular basis.

*The rewards.* Successful city managers have the satisfaction of performing a very complex job well. They also have the problem of pleasing several different politicians. One drawback is that advancement may require moving to new cities several times in a career.

Salaries vary widely, with larger cities paying the largest amounts. The median in 1998 was about $70,000 annually. City and county managers receive standard fringe benefits—such as vacation and sick leave—and many receive additional benefits, such as an automobile, moving expenses, and liability insurance.

*Where to find a job.* This is a small occupation, employing about 20,000 people including assistants. The major employers are cities ranging from 10,000 to 500,000 in population.

Information about this occupation is available from:

International City/County Management Association
777 North Capitol Street NE
Washington, DC 20002

## LEGISLATORS/COUNCIL MEMBERS

Making laws could be called the first function of government, for it is only after a society has agreed on the rules which govern it that the executive can enforce them and the judiciary can determine infractions of them. In fact, we had a legislature, the Continental Congress, even before we had a country.

The duties of city, county, or state legislator do not differ *in kind* from those of the most powerful senator in Washington. One might consider a multithousand dollar project to build a turn-lane at a busy intersection, while the other is concerned with the multibillion dollar interstate highway system, but both must strike a balance between the desirability of a government-provided service and the ability of the taxpayers to pay for it.

Relatively few of these jobs are full-time, year-round positions. State legislatures usually meet just part of the year; some meet only every other year. Governing boards of cities and counties are more likely to hold sessions throughout the year, meeting one day or evening every week or two, but—at least in theory—the board or council members work fewer than forty hours a week.

*What you should bring to this occupation.* Concern for the public welfare is probably the chief characteristic of these officials. Legislators and council members should be able to analyze complex issues and propose solutions. They must understand how their government operates, and they must be able to persuade others—both voters and other members of the body—to accept their ideas.

These are elected positions; the voters determine what experience, education, and ability are required. Most state legislators are management or professional workers; many are lawyers. Relatively few are clerical or blue-collar workers. Representatives from agriculture are relatively common in some areas, however, considering how few farmers there are in the economy as a whole.

*The rewards.* Successful legislators have the satisfaction of seeing their vision of society become reality, at least in part. They also experience the frustration of not being able to put all their plans into action.

Salaries and other benefits vary enormously. Annual salaries for state legislators range from no salary at all to more than $75,000. U.S. Senators and Representatives earned $136,700 per year in 1999.

*Where to learn more.* Attending public sessions of the governing board is one way to learn about these occupations. Working in a campaign is one of the best ways to learn what an election is like. The local government itself, the board of elections (or some similar body), and local political parties can provide information on the requirements for specific positions.

## ASSESSORS

Assessors evaluate taxable property. While the federal government raises most of its money from income taxes, a large proportion of state and local taxes is based on real estate or other property. Assessors determine the value of the property. They are usually elected or appointed by elected officials. Deputy assessors, or appraisers, however, are more likely to be merit system employees. They often have an associate or bachelor's degree with a major in real estate or assessing. In small towns, assessing may be a part-time job or even one of the duties of the town clerk.

Another area of employment is the court system. The federal government, as well as state and local governments, have three branches: *legislative, executive,* and *judicial.* Among the names used for parts of the judicial branch are supreme court, court of appeals, superior court, circuit court, and district court. Judges run the third branch—which administers the court system—and preside over trials, hearings, and grand jury proceedings. Other occupations in the judicial branch include bailiff or marshall, magistrate, court reporter, public defender, and court clerk. Typically, the judicial is the smallest branch of government in terms of employment and expenditures.

## JUDGES

Judges administer justice in our system of government. They control proceedings in the courtroom. In jury trials, they also interpret the law for the jury, explaining the possible verdicts, for example. In addition to presiding at trials, judges are also administrators. They are ultimately responsible for the smooth functioning of the judicial branch of government.

Judges usually work a standard forty-hour week in comfortable surroundings.

*What you should bring to this occupation.* Judges must be able to think clearly and analyze complex problems. They must also be able to win elections or impress those who do, since judges are either elected by the people or chosen by elected officials. They should possess extensive knowledge of law; and almost all have law degrees, although a degree requirement is not quite universal.

*The rewards.* Successful judges have the satisfaction of performing a difficult job well and contributing to the protection of society. They also have the problem of facing innumerable difficult decisions; both the wrongly condemned innocent person and the mistakenly freed criminal who attacks another victim weigh heavily on a conscientious judge's mind.

Federal judges earned a minimum of $125,800 in 1998, and some higher-level judges earned substantially more. Salaries of most state judges range from $79,400 to $113,300. Most judges enjoy better than average fringe benefits. Elected judges, however, have less job security than most government workers.

*Where to learn more.* You can best learn about this occupation by talking with a judge. Information about the careers of attorneys is also relevant.

## COURT REPORTERS

Court reporters are specialized stenographers who, using stenotype machines or shorthand, make word-for-word records of court proceedings, hearings, and legislative sessions. They may also be called shorthand reporters, hearing reporters, or legal reporters. A recording speed as high as 225 words per minute may be required, although 160 is sufficient for some jobs. Besides recording dictation, court reporters may also type, transcribe their notes, or dictate their notes for a typist; increasingly, however, the notes can be transcribed by computer. Shorthand reporters can learn their skills in two-year programs at post-high school technical institutes and junior colleges. Salaries are better than those of other clerical workers. This is a relatively small occupation for the clerical field, but demand is often greater than the supply. To learn more about this occupation, contact:

National Court Reporters Association
    8224 Old Courthouse Road
    Vienna, VA 22182

## LAWYERS

Attorneys are employed in substantial numbers in federal agencies and state and local governments. They are an integral part of the criminal justice system and may work for a state attorney general or in county courts as prosecutors or public defenders. Some jobs in these offices are filled by recent law school graduates who need to gain some experience, or need immediate employment to begin paying back educational loans. Many recent graduates do not have the funds to open a private practice, and if they can't get quick placement in a law firm, they turn to these jobs to get started. It is also an excellent training ground for young lawyers who envision a career in elective office. The workings of a state's attorney's office are often high-profile and will make those who work there familiar names and faces to the public.

In addition, the almost twenty-thousand municipalities in the United States employ large numbers of lawyers who help develop local statutes, interpret federal and state regulations, establish enforcement procedures, and argue cases on behalf of the city. Smaller communities may retain lawyers who also have a practice that allows them time to work on contract. Special districts, school districts, and townships will also either have their own lawyers or contract on a per hour basis.

Still other lawyers may work for nonprofit organizations, trade associations, contracting and consulting firms, and lobbying groups. While none of these categories is actually employed by governments, they often work with legislatures developing laws, conducting research, and contracting for other services.

*What you should bring to this occupation.* First, of course, you must have completed your degree at an accredited law school and then have passed the bar examination. After completing the first phase you must then bring your skills in managing people, communicating both orally and in written papers, and some specialized technical knowledge to your work. Computers have moved into the world of law in a grand style. Lawyers now own software that substitutes to some degree for the long hours in law libraries. They will then use a computer to organize and index the material their software has led them to. Tax lawyers make wide use of computers to make computations and to explore various tax strategies. Finally, lawyers must be capable of an extreme degree of discretion in terms of keeping clients' legal affairs in the strictest of confidence. Trading war stories about interesting, but confidential, cases is not an option that a good lawyer has.

*The rewards.* Lawyers are well-paid professionals whose working conditions, incomes, and opportunities for variety in their work are exceptionally high. There is no problem of their work being seasonal, and, curiously enough, the harder times get—the more lawyers are needed to deal with such events as bankruptcies, divorces, and foreclosures. While law practices are not totally recession-proof, they are often among the last to feel economic stress.

*Where to learn more.* For more information, contact:

American Bar Association
750 North Lake Shore Drive
Chicago, IL 60611

Law School Admission Council
P.O. Box 40
Newtown, PA 18940

In 1998, the median annual salary for all lawyers was $78,170. For those employed in government, the median was $36,000 six months after graduation, and substantially higher with more experience. Whether they go on to private practice, elective office, or judgeships, lawyers will be among the top occupations in annual income within a decade after leaving law school.

## PARALEGALS

Lawyers are increasingly working with paralegals—sometimes called *legal assistants.* There is much work to be done in law offices that does not require a law school graduate. In general, paralegals will do research and background work for lawyers. As costs increase, more and more legal departments in state and local government have only a few lawyers and dozens of paralegals in their employ.

In government, paralegals will analyze legal materials for use within the office, maintain reference files, conduct research, collect and analyze evidence for hearings, and prepare informational material for their own office use and for the public.

*What you should bring to this occupation.* Some lawyers will prefer to train their own assistants, or to promote the most capable legal secretaries in the office. Some will search for employees who have completed formal educational programs for the occupation. Paralegals need not be certified, but the National Association of Legal Assistants has established standards for voluntary certification.

Paralegals must be skilled in dealing with clients, follow the same ethical guidelines as lawyers in terms of confidentially, have excellent speaking and writing skills, and have an ability to work conscientiously, although unsupervised.

*The rewards.* Paralegals enjoy interesting work done in pleasant surroundings, better than average salaries for office workers, and the respect of family and friends. The median annual salary in 1998 was $32,760. There is, however, little opportunity to rise to a higher position. Paralegals cannot just start practicing law—unless, of course, they learn to like the work enough to enroll in law school. For more information, contact:

American Association for Paralegal Education
   P.O. Box 40244
   Overland Park, KS 66204

National Association of Legal Assistants, Inc.
   1516 South Boston Street
   Tulsa, OK 74119

Standing Committee on Legal Assistants
   American Bar Association
   750 North Lake Shore Drive
   Chicago, IL 60611

# CHAPTER 10

# POLICE AND CORRECTION JOBS

Police protection is a major task of the local government, with no function other than education employing so many workers. State governments and federal agencies also employ large numbers of law enforcement personnel. In 1998, police officers and detectives held approximately 764,000 jobs. Police officers investigate crimes, arrest suspects, and direct traffic. In large cities, individual police officers usually specialize in one kind of work. In small towns, they do a little bit of everything. Much of the work is routine, but some people are attracted to the job because a routine patrol can suddenly turn into a hot pursuit.

State police are organized in several different ways. State police departments typically provide full police services for unincorporated areas of the state. Highway patrols chiefly enforce traffic laws and assist motorists who have been in an accident or who have other problems. However the distinctions are not always clear. Arizona and Texas, for example, have highway patrols within their state police departments. Hawaii has neither a state police department nor a highway patrol.

Hiring standards and evaluation procedures for state departments are similar to those of city departments.

## POLICE OFFICERS

Television and motion picture cops and robbers bear little resemblance to real policemen. Most officers are assigned to patrol or traffic control duties. Boredom is often the norm. Patrolling a neighborhood enables officers to know what activities are normal, so that they can spot the unusual; it also tends to prevent crime. At any time, patrol officers may be called upon to stop a burglary, quiet a disturbance, or save a life. Traffic officers direct traffic, give out tickets, and deal with accidents.

Police departments also have divisions that specialize in investigations of certain types of crimes, such as burglaries or homicides, or in other activities, such as juvenile affairs. Other special units are motorcycle patrols, mobile rescue teams, and helicopter divisions. Officers may also be assigned to crime laboratories, record divisions, or police clerk duties.

No matter what their assignment, police officers spend much of their time completing reports of incidents. These reports can serve to build a case or indicate a problem. They are also needed because another important duty of officers is to testify in court.

Officers usually work forty hours a week, but not from nine to five, Monday to Friday. Police protection must be provided every hour of the day, every day of the year. Consequently, officers work unusual shifts, including most holidays. Furthermore, they are usually on call twenty-four hours a day in case a sudden emergency arises. Officers must also be prepared to work outdoors in all kinds of weather.

*What you should bring to this occupation.* Successful police officers, to paraphrase Kipling, can keep their heads when all around them are losing theirs. They are also able both to follow orders and to take charge of a situation. They enjoy working with others.

Many cities have a maximum age limit for job entry of about thirty-five. Most require that applicants be at least twenty-one years old; some departments hire police cadets, however, who are younger. A high school diploma is almost always required, and some departments look for applicants with at least some college education, often in fields such as law enforcement or the administration of justice.

Prospective police recruits are evaluated in many different ways. A background investigation, medical examination, and interview are almost universal. Psychological evaluation, polygraph testing, physical performance tests, and written tests are also used by many departments. Interviews are designed to determine whether you are highly motivated and can keep calm under pressure. You should learn exactly what is required and practice for all the different types of tests to learn early if you have any disqualifying conditions.

Training usually begins at a police academy run by the department or the state; academy training lasts six months in New York. It combines physical conditioning and self-defense with the study of law and police procedure. First aid and marksmanship are also learned and practiced. Training continues when a recruit is assigned to a station. And evaluation continues during both training and a probationary period.

*The rewards.* Police officers experience satisfaction from preventing crimes and ensuring the safety of their fellow citizens. Among the drawbacks of the occupation are that a great deal of paperwork is required, the danger of injury and death is ever present, and the fight against crime is never won.

Police officers advance by being promoted through the ranks. Additional testing usually takes place at every rank. Officers may also become more specialized in their work, concentrating on one type of police activity.

The median salary in 1998 for police patrol officers was $37,710, according to the Bureau of Labor Statistics. Sheriffs and deputy sheriffs earned median annual salaries of $28,270. Federal law enforcement officers earned salaries starting at more than $34,000 and progressing to more than $60,000 annually. Officers receive the usual fringe benefits plus a uniform or uniform allowance and required equipment, including weapons. Because of the agility that officers must have, many departments have pension plans that permit an officer to retire after twenty or twenty-five years of service at half pay.

*Where to find a job.* More than a half million people work as local police officers and detectives; they are ten times more numerous than state police officers.

These occupations are projected to grow more slowly than average during the next decade, in part because of the use of civilian technicians to perform specialized duties once performed by officers. Turnover is also relatively low for this occupation. However, because of the occupation's size, a great many openings will become available. If the past is any guide, competition for those openings will be keen.

*Where to learn more.* Your local police department and state police department or highway patrol are the best places to obtain precise information on job requirements, salaries, and test schedules.

Contact the nearest FBI office for information about employment with that agency. Other sources of information include:

United States Marshalls Service
  Field Staffing Branch
  600 Army Navy Drive
  Arlington, VA 22220

U.S. Border Patrol
  Chester A. Arthur Building
  425 I Street NW
  Washington, DC 20536

## OTHER POLICE PROTECTION OCCUPATIONS

*Crossing guards* ensure the safety of children at busy intersections before and after school. A high school diploma is usually required; good character is important, and extensive background checks are often performed. For more information, contact a local police department.

*Detectives* gather evidence for criminal cases. They interview witnesses and suspects, keep watch over suspects, and assist in arrests. Most have several years' experience as police officers before becoming detectives. Detectives usually earn more than police officers. To learn more about this occupation, consult the sources of information listed under police officers.

*Dispatchers* who work for police departments, fire departments, and hospitals receive telephone and radio calls from people seeking assistance and broadcast the necessary information to field units. They also keep records, or logs, of the calls they receive and the action they take. A high school education is usually required of these workers and, frequently, an FCC radio license. About 248,000 people work as police, fire, and ambulance dispatchers. Local governments employ most of these workers.

*Police clerks* perform various clerical tasks to keep the police department functioning smoothly. They keep records, order supplies, run computers, and operate switchboards. A high school diploma is usually required. Related positions include those of administrative assistants, keyboarders, and word processors for local governments in justice, public order, and safety. To learn more about this occupation, contact local police departments.

*Sheriffs* combine the duties of a police chief and warden because the county sheriff's department is responsible for traffic control, criminal investigations, and jailing prisoners in the county's jurisdiction. In some states—California, for example—sheriffs also act as coroners. Sheriffs are elected in most states.

Salaries of sheriffs vary widely, depending in part upon the size of the county they work for. This is a relatively small occupation, since by definition there can be only one sheriff in a county, no matter how many deputies there are. Deputy sheriffs are grouped with police officers as a vocational category. To learn more about this occupation, consult your local sheriff's office.

*State highway patrol officers* are chiefly responsible for traffic control on major highways. Officers also perform regular police functions in unincorporated parts of a state. In general, officers must meet the same standards as police officers in city departments. Salaries are comparable to those of police officers.

## CORRECTION DEPARTMENTS

Correction departments run prisons and jails and supervise parolees. They employ administrators and food service, health, and maintenance workers, although many of these duties are performed by inmates. The largest group of employees is made up of the correction officers or prison guards. They are employed by the federal government, state governments, and cities and counties.

### Correction Officers

Clanging doors and lonely watchtowers mark the working atmosphere of the correction officers who guard prisoners in state penitentiaries and local jails. Their jobs entail keeping careful watch over the prisoners at all times, whether from towers and guardrooms or while escorting them from place to place. They inspect the prison, checking for signs of damage to locks, doors, and windows and for unsafe or unhealthy conditions. Correction officers also supplement the efforts of psychologists and social workers.

Correction officers usually work an eight-hour day, five days a week, but their shifts may include holidays, weekends, and nights. The working conditions largely depend on the prison environment.

*What you should bring to this occupation.* Correction officers must have good judgment; they must be able to think and act quickly and effectively.

The usual educational requirement is a high school diploma. Applicants must usually be at least eighteen years of age, and take a series of tests including a written examination and a test of physical agility. A medical examination may also be required.

Once hired, new officers receive one to six months of training.

*The rewards.* Correction officers have the satisfaction of protecting society; however, the job can be both stressful and hazardous. They can advance through promotion to sergeant or transfer to a related occupation such as a probation or parole officer, although such a change may require additional education.

The median salary for correction officers employed by state governments was $27,300 in 1997 and $29,700 for those employed by local governments. Federal correction officers averaged $32,600. They receive standard fringe benefits, and housing is sometimes provided.

*Where to find a job.* Roughly 360,000 correction officers work for state and local governments, and about 12,000 are employed in federal institutions. About half work at state penitentiaries and the rest at local jails.

*Where to learn more.* The following organizations can provide further information:

The American Jail Association
   2053 Day Road
   Hagerstown, MD 21740

International Association of Correctional Officers
   P.O. Box 81826
   Lincoln, NE 68501

## Other Correction Occupations

*Parole officers* work with the correction or parole department. Parolees are criminals who have been released from prison before completing their sentences. Early release provides an incentive for good behavior and enables the department to see if people can adjust to society while it still has some control over them. Parole officers keep track of the parolees, make certain that parole rules are obeyed, and help parolees make this adjustment by assisting them in their search for job training and employment or in other ways. Parole officers usually have a bachelor's degree in sociology, psychology, criminology, or correction, and experience in the correction department. Their salaries are comparable to those of social workers; the average salary for social workers is in the lower third for all wage earners.

*Probation officers* work within the court system, although they are employees of the state correction agency. Before a trial, they investigate the accused person's family background and position in the community in order to recommend whether or not a judge should grant bail. Before a person is sentenced, the officer conducts a similar investigation to see if probation rather than prison should be imposed. After sentencing, officers supervise people on probation to ensure that they obey the rules of their sentences. Probation officers usually have a bachelor's degree in sociology, psychology, criminology, or correction, and experience in the department where they work.

## CHAPTER 11

# COMPUTER JOBS

State and local governmental units have lagged behind private employers in their use of computers and computer systems mainly because they have had to await legislative approval to spend the monies to get "on-line." However, most governmental units—even the smallest and most rural—have now come into the computer age. We are reducing the number of clerical positions in government because of the increased productivity the new technology provides. At the same time, from data-entry operator to systems programmer, the opportunities for computer-related jobs are many because of the sheer size of the occupation.

## PROGRAMMERS, SYSTEMS ANALYSTS, OPERATORS

Programmers write detailed descriptions of the steps a computer must follow to solve a problem. After designing the program, the programmer will run sample data through the system to determine if it works correctly or if it needs some adjustments. Programmers then prepare instructions for the operator who will run the program. Programmers may work alone on a project, or, in the case of large projects, may be part of a team.

Computer programmers usually work from descriptions of a problem presented to them by a systems analyst. In some instances, the jobs may be combined and the job will be titled *programmer-analyst.* Others who work in the field include: *data entry clerks, database managers,* and *computer service technicians.* Most technicians are employed by the manufacturers of the equipment, but some employers, where there is a large enough installation to warrant it, hire their own.

*What you should bring to this occupation.* There are no standard training requirements for computer-related jobs. Depending on the work to be done and the salary you expect to earn, you can come minimally prepared, or you can come with advanced degrees in computer science, mathematics, or engineering.

Computer programming, system analysis, and other courses can be found in high schools, community colleges, vocational and technical schools, colleges, and universities. There are also Internet-based and home-study courses available. Be prepared to take courses throughout your career. This is an area in which the technology changes very quickly. Courses are offered by employers, by software vendors, and by computer manufacturers. If you expect to advance in your job, get used to the idea of being a periodic student.

*The rewards.* There are well-paying jobs in all parts of the country. In fact, there are opportunities for experienced people internationally. A job in state or local government could mean preparation for a fascinating job in the private sector. The work is usually done in clean, well-lighted, pleasant surroundings. The opportunities for further training and advancement are many. Most people in the field will work standard workweeks, but occasionally will have to work on weekends when the equipment is not needed for scheduled work.

*Where to find a job.* Your Job Service office will have openings listed, as will your local or state offices. Watch newspapers for announcements of openings. Search as you would for any other possibility. Additional sources of information are listed below:

Association for Computing Machinery
    1515 Broadway
    New York, NY 10036

Institute for Certification of Computing Professionals
    2200 East Devon Avenue
    Des Plaines, IL 60018

The ability to think logically, to be patient, and to enjoy the challenge of being unusually accurate will be necessary if you are to find success in the computer world. If those attributes are yours, your horizons are wide open—particularly if you are ambitious and flexible enough to enjoy change. The salary level is also up to you. You may enter at a salary as low as $27,000, but continuing study will take you into the higher reaches of salaried employment.

## CHAPTER 12

# EDUCATION

In this country, public education is primarily the responsibility of state and local governments. It is also by far the major source of state and local government employment, accounting for almost half of all jobs. Except in Hawaii—which has a state-run school system—elementary schools and high schools are run by local governments. Community colleges and public universities are usually under the control of the state, though they may be largely self-governing. In addition to the schools themselves, each state also has a department of education that sets standards, such as the minimum qualifications for teachers; establishes the curriculum or subjects to be taught; and determines the school calendar. The local school district, community college, or university hires the teachers, puts up new schools and buildings, closes old ones, and prepares the budget.

Education has the lion's share—the whale's share would be more accurate—of government workers. It employs administrators (such as principals), service and maintenance workers, clerical workers, and, of course, teachers. Job titles include: adult education teacher, building custodian, college and university teacher, counselor, general clerk, institutional cook, kindergarten and elementary school teacher, kitchen helper, librarian, library assistant, maintenance repairer, principal, school bus driver, secondary school teacher, secretary, teacher aide, typist, and vocational education teacher. Many of these occupations are discussed below; some are treated in other chapters.

The day we met our first teacher, we little suspected how many administrators were needed to bring us together. There are generally three administrative layers in each state's school system.

At the top, usually, is the *state board,* which sets policies, including the curriculum; whether the policies are fairly general or highly specific varies a good deal. In some cases, the state even picks the textbooks. The chief administrator at the state level may be known as the commissioner of education, commissioner of public instruction, or by some other title. This person is elected in some states and appointed by elected officials in others.

The middle administrative layer is the *school district,* which may have as many as eight hundred schools. It, too, usually has a governing board to make final decisions, such as deciding on the budget or determining if the number of teachers and schools is too high or too low. The board is either elected or appointed by elected officials. The day-to-day running of the district is left to the *superintendent.* Besides seeing that the board's decisions are carried out, the superintendent also continually reassesses the needs of the district in order to report them to the board. In larger districts, the superintendent may have several assistants, each of whom is responsible for a group of high schools, middle schools, and elementary schools, or for certain functions throughout the district, such as construction and renovation or teacher evaluation.

The basic administrative unit is the individual school, which is managed by a principal.

## SCHOOL PRINCIPALS

The principal runs the school in accordance with the rules and policies established by the school board and the superintendent.

Principals assign teachers, set schedules, and coordinate school activities. They supervise the maintenance and cafeteria staffs and, of course, the teachers. In a single day, a principal might meet with a teacher concerning an unruly student, go over needed repairs with the custodian, visit a classroom to observe a teacher in action, conduct an assembly, work on next year's budget, counsel a student, and confer with a group of parents about plans for a computer literacy program.

*What you should bring to this occupation. Principal* is short for "principal teacher," and the chief characteristics of successful principals are the same as those of good teachers: they love children and they love to watch them grow in knowledge and confidence. Principals also need the attributes of any good manager: organization and leadership skills, self-confidence, and decisiveness.

Public school principals must be certified by the state. Almost all have teaching experience and graduate school training, such as a master's degree in school administration, which includes such courses as school management, school law, school finance and budgeting, personnel administration, and community relations.

*The rewards.* Administration does not offer the immediate satisfactions of teaching. However, principals gain satisfaction from performing a complicated job well and contributing to the education of students. On the other hand, they are subject to criticism from all sides and face innumerable difficult choices in the allocation of the school's resources.

The following, according to the Educational Research Service, were the average salaries in 1997–98. Elementary school: $64,653; junior high or middle school: $68,740; senior high school: $74,380. Principals receive standard fringe benefits of state and local government workers, although they do not receive the longer vacations of teachers.

*Where to learn more.* These organizations can supply more information about school principals:

Your state's department of education

American Association of School Administrators
    1801 North Moore Street
    Arlington, VA 22209

American Federation of School Administrators
    1729 Twenty-first Street NW
    Washington, DC 20009

The National Association of Elementary School Principals
    1615 Duke Street
    Alexandria, VA 22314

## ELEMENTARY AND SECONDARY SCHOOL TEACHERS

"If you can read this, thank a teacher." Perhaps you have seen that bumper sticker. The same message could be printed across the cover of every book, newspaper, magazine, and pamphlet that has ever taught you something or entertained you.

We are all familiar with what teachers do in the classroom: They present new information, conduct exercises and tests, and maintain order. Much of their work takes place outside the classroom, however, preparing lessons, grading papers, increasing their knowledge, and attending meetings.

In the classroom, teachers have different duties depending on their specialty. Broadly speaking, elementary school teachers are responsible for all academic subjects while secondary school teachers usually instruct students in a single subject. Even at the lowest grades, however, some division of labor takes place. For example, physical education is almost always conducted by a teacher trained for that subject. English as a second language, special education, music, and art are other specialties within elementary education. As for high school, a secondary school specialist looks like a generalist to a college professor. Social studies teachers in high school, for example, may be called on to teach history, geography, economics, or sociology, all of which are distinct major fields in college. And a college professor who teaches only medieval English literature would be hard pressed to handle the combination of grammar, literature, and composition that a high school teacher must contend with.

Teachers work when schools are open, which is for about 7 hours at least 180 days a year in most states. They also work when schools are closed, as indicated above. The average workweek may be longer than forty hours. Working conditions in schools vary widely with regard to heating, air conditioning, lighting, and toilet facilities. More important to most teachers is the variation in class size, resulting from the failure of communities to provide enough teachers and classrooms to have children in class-size groups.

*What you should bring to this occupation.* Successful teachers love children. They are also creative, intellectually curious, and patient. It goes without saying that they need extraordinary communicating skills with both individuals and groups.

Public school teachers must be certified. The basic educational requirement is a bachelor's degree. College graduates who did not take education courses can sometimes meet the requirements through graduate school study.

Besides education, requirements might include citizenship, good health, and good character. Recently, some states have begun to require that new teachers pass competence tests. About half the states require that teachers earn a master's degree within a certain number of years after being hired.

*The rewards.* The light shining from the face of a child who has just grasped a new idea is, perhaps, the greatest satisfaction of teaching. Teachers in most school systems also enjoy a good deal of independence. Drawbacks of the profession include relatively low salaries for the amount of education required, a loss of prestige in the last generation, and extensive paperwork that can lessen contact time with students. Some teachers also complain about the difficulty of maintaining order and discipline in the classroom.

Teachers can advance by becoming administrators or specialists such as counselors. Both moves require further education. In fact, most teachers remain in teaching.

The median annual salary for teachers ranged from $33,590 to $37,890 in 1998. They receive the usual fringe benefits and more vacation time than most workers. They do not get quite as much time off as they seem to, however, because of their need to continue their own education and improve their skills.

*Where to find a job.* Elementary, middle, and secondary schools employ more than three million classroom teachers.

The job outlook for teachers currently is excellent. Population growth and the retirement of large numbers of teachers is expected to bring an increased demand for qualified teachers in the years ahead.

*Where to learn more.* Contact your local school district and state department of education and other districts or states where you might wish to work to learn the precise requirements for certification in the subjects you wish to teach.

Many teachers are members of associations and unions such as the following:

American Federation of Teachers
555 New Jersey Avenue NW
Washington, DC 20001

National Education Association
1201 Sixteenth Street NW
Washington, DC 20036

A list of accredited schools of education is available from the following association:

National Council for Accreditation of Teacher Education
2010 Massachusetts Avenue NW
Washington, DC 20036

## COOKS

Institutional cooks prepare food in large quantities. As they gain experience, they also order food and other supplies, keep records, and supervise kitchen helpers.

Their day might start very early, so they can prepare breakfasts, or run late, so they can clean up after dinner; weekend work is also required for some jobs. Most institutional cooks in government, however, work in elementary and secondary schools, where few breakfasts and no suppers are served; these cooks work only on school days.

Cooks are subject to extreme heat from ovens, steam from boiling pots or dishwashers, and cold from walk-in refrigerators. They are on their feet much of the time.

*What you should bring to this occupation.* Cooks should have a good sense of taste and smell. They must be able to plan their day carefully so that meals will be ready at the proper time.

A high school diploma is sufficient for most entry-level positions, although some employers prefer new workers who have earned an associate's degree with courses in subjects such as food preparation or menu planning. Experience working in an institutional or restaurant kitchen is likely to impress an employer more than education, however. A health certificate may be required to screen out people with contagious diseases. New workers are usually trained on the job.

*The rewards.* Cooks have the satisfaction of seeing a job through from beginning to end. Not always having the best quality material to work with because of the need to keep the average cost per meal low may be frustrating. In 1998, average hourly wages for all cooks were $7.81. Those employed in elementary and secondary schools averaged $7.16 per hour, and those in hospitals earned an average hourly wage of $7.55. Cooks enjoy the usual fringe benefits.

*Where to find a job.* This is a large occupation, employing more than 3.3 million people, including large numbers in schools, hospitals, and government agencies. The major employers by far are schools. Hospitals also employ institutional cooks, as do nursing homes, child-care services, and jails and prisons. Employment growth in state and local governments will depend most upon growth of the elementary school population and the growth of hospital employment.

*Where to learn more.* The following associations may be helpful:

American Culinary Federation
P.O. Box 3466
St. Augustine, FL 32085

The National Restaurant Association
1200 Seventeenth Street NW
Washington, DC 20036

## OTHER EDUCATION OCCUPATIONS

*Athletic coaches* teach individuals and groups how to play different sports and how to improve their performance. They also may select team members, purchase equipment, and organize events. High school coaches usually have teaching duties as well. They must, therefore, be certified teachers, most often in physical education. Their salaries are comparable with those of other teachers. One point should be made: Competition is usually keen for coaching jobs. To learn more about this occupation, you can contact unions or associations such as the National High School Athletic Coaches Association, P.O. Box 4342, Hamden, CT 06514.

*College professors* teach, conduct research, and perform administrative duties. The proportion of time spent on any one activity varies. College teachers are responsible for specialized subjects, the degree of specialization increasing with the size of the school and its involvement with graduate education. A master's degree is sufficient for some positions; the Ph.D. is usually preferred and often required, however. The average salary for college professors in public institutions in 1999–2000 was $57,686, according to the American Association of University Professors. Salaries are lower than the average for the occupation in fine and liberal arts; they are higher in engineering, mathematics, and some other scientific fields. The outlook is complicated by the high degree of specialization required; faculty members trained in one discipline are not qualified to teach in another. As a result, colleges may be unable to find enough teachers for certain subjects, such as engineering, while job hunters cannot find any openings in another field.

*Counselors* in schools help students deal with personal or family problems, choose courses, and decide what they will do after graduation. They work closely with teachers, school nurses, and school psychologists. School counselors usually have one to five years of education after college. Teaching experience is usually, but not always, required. Median annual earnings for counselors employed in elementary and secondary schools were $42,100 in 1998 and $34,700 for those working in colleges and universities. About 182,000 counselors were employed in 1998. To learn more you can contact the American Counseling Association, 5999 Stevenson Avenue, Alexandria, VA 22304.

Counselors work in many settings other than schools, such as job service offices and social services agencies. Information on these positions is also available from the association listed above.

*Speech pathologists* work with people who have trouble speaking because of a problem such as a cleft palate, a lisp, or a stutter. They diagnose the problem and plan a course of action, such as teaching the person new ways to use their lips. A master's degree in speech-language pathology is usually required for these workers, although a bachelor's degree is sufficient in some cases. A teaching certificate or certificate to practice speech-language pathology may also be required. In 1998, median annual earnings of speech-language pathologists and audiologists were $43,080, according to the U.S. Department of Labor. This is a relatively small occupation with a total employment of about 105,000. Employers include schools, clinics, and hospitals. To learn more you can contact:

American Speech-Language-Hearing Association
   10801 Rockville Pike
   Rockville, MD 20852

*Teacher assistants* help teachers by taking care of clerical and housekeeping tasks and also help with instruction by working with individual students or small groups. A high school education is sufficient for some positions, but employers prefer at least some college if the person will work with students on lessons. The median hourly wage was $7.61 in 1998. This is a fairly large occupation, employing about 1.2 million people. About half these workers are part-time employees, and most work in the primary grades.

## CHAPTER 13

# FIRE PROTECTION

Fire protection refers to the work of fire departments: putting out fires, conducting inspections, running fire safety programs, and—in many cases—providing emergency medical assistance. Fire departments employ dispatchers, clerks, fire inspectors, fire marshals, and emergency medical technicians. Naturally, the largest occupation is firefighter.

## FIREFIGHTERS

How many heroes are there in America? At least 314,000. That's the number of firefighters now employed, most working for state and local governments. Firefighters are among the most respected employees of local governments. No one questions their courage or the importance of their work.

A firefighter's main duty is to put out fires, obviously enough. All firefighters must also be prepared to rescue victims and give first aid.

Firefighters average a 50-hour week; they also have unusual shifts. Some work 24 hours and then have 48 hours off; others work 10 hours for three days and have 2 days off. Still other variations are possible.

To become a firefighter, you must usually pass a long series of tests. You begin by submitting an application. If you meet certain minimum qualifications, you will be scheduled to take the first of the tests. Minimum qualifications might include age (usually at least twenty-one and often no more than thirty-five, although many departments have no upper limit) and residency.

You may have to take as many as five different kinds of tests and different kinds of examinations.

Next comes a test of strength and physical agility. The parts of the test are related to a firefighter's actual duties. You can learn precisely what tests are given by the departments that you want to work for.

Interviews are another kind of test. At the interview, experienced firefighters will ask you a series of questions to learn why you want to enter the occupation and what steps you have taken to prepare for it. The board is less concerned about your specific answers than your attitude and personality; they want to see if you keep calm under pressure, follow instructions, express yourself clearly, and are highly motivated.

Medical examinations for firefighters are stringent. Learn the exact standards for any department you might want to work for before you even apply. Many companies use the National Fire Protection Association's standards. You can obtain a copy of it from the address below and have your own physician examine you so you'll know if you meet the medical qualifications. Among the disqualifying physical conditions are color blindness, poor vision, heart trouble, and back trouble.

Background investigations are conducted by some fire departments, who check for a criminal record, serious driving violations, and credit problems.

Firefighters are usually trained by the department after being hired. A few departments have formal apprenticeship programs.

*The rewards.* Firefighters receive a great deal of satisfaction from their job, which offers extreme challenges and the immediate reward of saving human lives. Prospective firefighters should also realize that the risk of injury and even death is ever present.

The median annual salary of firefighters was $31,170 in 1998, according to the U.S. Department of Labor. Firefighters are provided with protective clothing by the department and may receive a uniform or uniform allowance. They generally enjoy the usual fringe benefits. Because of the agility needed to perform their duties, firefighters often are able to retire early; in some cases, they can retire at half pay after twenty years.

This is a moderate-size occupation, numbering about 314,000. The number of openings projected is smaller than would be expected for an occupation of this size for two reasons. First, turnover is extremely low, an indication of the high degree of satisfaction firefighters have with their jobs. Second, only slow growth in employment is projected. Competition for firefighter positions is usually keen.

The following organizations can provide career information on firefighters:

Your local fire department

International Association of Fire Chiefs
  4025 Fair Ridge Drive
  Fairfax, VA 22033

International Association of Fire Fighters
  1750 New York Avenue NW
  Washington, DC 20006

National Fire Protection Association
  P.O. Box 9101
  Quincy, MA 02269

## ANOTHER FIRE DEPARTMENT OCCUPATION: EMERGENCY MEDICAL TECHNICIAN

Emergency medical technicians (EMT's) may work as dispatchers, ambulance attendants, or paramedics. The paramedics are the most highly trained. Both ambulance and paramedic EMT's give first aid to victims of auto accidents, heart attacks, shootings, and other emergencies. Paramedics are able to give aid that requires more complex medical procedures, such as administering intravenous drugs under the supervision of a physician. Ambulance work requires at least one hundred hours of training in a course approved by the U.S. Department of Transportation; training for paramedics takes from four to six times as long. To learn more about this occupation, contact:

National Association of Emergency Medical Technicians
  408 Monroe Street
  Clinton, MS 39056

## CHAPTER 14

# HEALTH AND HOSPITAL JOBS

Health is not just the concern of the hospitals. The public health department is usually responsible for preventing the spread of diseases. To do their job, they employ health and regulatory inspectors as well as health professionals. The inspectors check restaurants, grocery stores, and other public places. The health professionals—mostly nurses—work at clinics giving shots and providing information on pregnancy and common health problems. A clinic or local health department can range in size from hundreds of employees to just a few: public health nurse, sanitarian, and clerical worker. Schools also employ public health nurses. State governments employ a little less than half the workers, and counties about one-fourth of them. Among the agencies in this category are public health agencies, mental health agencies, maternity and child care programs, immunization programs, communicable disease programs, and environmental health programs.

## PUBLIC HEALTH NURSES

Many public health nurses work to prevent illness by providing information, health screening, and medications such as vaccines.

Public health nurses also care for the injured and ill, either in a clinic or as visiting nurses.

Public health nurses usually work a forty-hour week. Evening hours are required at some clinics. Nurses in schools work mostly when the schools are open.

Conditions in clinics and schools are similar in that both are indoors and have ready access to medical supplies. Visiting nurses encounter many more varied conditions and must travel throughout the day despite the weather.

*What you should bring to this occupation.* Public health nurses must be able to care for all types of people and make sound decisions in the midst of an emergency. More than average stamina may be needed, especially by visiting nurses.

A license is required of fully qualified public health nurses. To obtain the license, a bachelor of science degree in nursing is usually required. Degree programs usually take four to five years; they should not be confused with associate degree programs that usually take two years. People with associate degrees may complete the requirements to become registered nurses but not fully qualified public health nurses in most cases.

*The rewards.* The satisfaction of public health nursing, like that of other nursing fields, is helping to make people well. Public health nurses also enjoy greater independence on the job than most nurses do. Like other nurses, public health nurses must accept the reality of chronic illness and death.

In 1998, the median salary was $40,690, according to the U.S. Department of Labor.

*Where to find a job.* Nurses held over two million jobs in 1998. Many worked for local governments in public and community health agencies. Other major employers are local health departments and clinics. Three percent of all registered nurses worked in schools.

Nursing is a rapidly growing occupation. The combination of fast growth and large size means that many thousands of jobs should become available in the near future. For more information, contact:

American Public Health Association
   800 I Street NW
   Washington, DC 20001

American School Health Association
   Box 708
   Kent, OH 44240

## HEALTH INSPECTORS

Rats, roaches, and rancid cheese are among the less pleasant things in the world; health inspectors try to keep them among the less common. Inspectors usually specialize. *Consumer safety inspectors* check up on food, drugs, and other products, or weights and measures. For example, they might look for mislabeled packages or signs of decomposition or contamination in a product. *Food inspectors* work with veterinarians at meat packing plants, ensuring that the animals and the plant meet state standards. *Environmental health inspectors* or *sanitarians* check some processing plants, such as dairies, but they also ensure that restaurants, hospitals, and other places that serve food are kept clean and free of vermin. They must also do field work and write reports.

Inspectors usually work a standard forty-hour week. Much of their time is spent at inspection sites, working either alone or as part of a team.

*What you should bring to this occupation.* Inspectors must be able to accept responsibility for their decisions, which can have serious consequences. On the one hand, the duties of their work can close down a business; on the other hand, failure to enforce health codes can result in illness or death. Inspectors must be experts in the field they are going to work in, and they must get along well with a wide range of people under somewhat difficult circumstances.

The education required depends on the specialty. Sanitarians must usually have a bachelor's degree in environmental health or a physical or biological science.

Most states require that environmental health inspectors or sanitarians be licensed.

Employers train new workers in the laws that concern their work and departmental procedures.

*The rewards.* Inspectors have the satisfaction of contributing to the health of their communities. The constant need to attend to minute details and the possibility of confrontations with restaurant owners or others can be stressful, however.

According to the U.S. Department of Labor, average annual earnings for inspectors and compliance officers was $36,820 in 1998. For those working for the federal government, starting salaries ranged from $25,500 to $31,200 in 1999.

*Where to find a job.* About 176,000 people worked as inspectors and compliance officers in 1998. Average growth is projected for these occupations through 2008.

*Where to learn more.* The following association can provide further information about this occupation:

Institute of Food Technologists
221 North LaSalle Street
Chicago, IL 60601

## HOMEMAKER/HOME HEALTH AIDES

Home health aides, also sometimes called "homemakers," will become a bigger and bigger category of workers in the coming decade. By all indicators, the older population will continue to increase and will need home health and homemaking services in increasing amounts. In addition, as the cost of health care skyrockets, more patients will be treated in the home to try to control those costs. Further, new technology is making home care increasingly possible. For example, portable versions of many machines, formerly only available in the hospital, are already in use in the home. For further information about this rapidly growing field, write to:

The National Association for Home Care
227 Seventh Street SE
Washington, DC 20003

## HOSPITAL JOBS

Hospitals employ some of the best-paid workers in the country—doctors—and some of the poorest-paid—nursing aides and orderlies. In between come a host of other people: clinical laboratory technicians, general clerks, hospital administrators, kitchen helpers, licensed practical nurses, medical laboratory technologists, registered nurses, psychiatric aides, radiological technicians, secretaries, and other workers. The operation of public hospitals is the largest single function of state and local governments after education.

About half the hospitals in the country are public. Local hospitals are often general hospitals, which means they care for all sorts of injuries and illnesses. Some state hospitals are long-term psychiatric hospitals, serving the retarded and mentally ill. A trend toward smaller, residential facilities, group homes, and other less restricted environments for these patients has reduced the staffs of these hospitals, although they are still major employers.

## Registered Nurses

The needs of the patient and the instructions of the patient's doctor determine most of the duties of the nurse. Nurses give people shots, test blood pressure, and bandage wounds, keeping records of everything they do. Some nurses spend their day caring for bedridden patients who, besides medical care, need help with eating and with personal hygiene. Other nurses are primarily concerned with supervising orderlies, nurse aides, licensed practical nurses, and technicians.

Hours and working conditions for nurses vary. Nursing care must be provided 24 hours a day, so many nurses work nights and weekends. Although an 8-hour, 5-day week is still fairly standard, it is not universal. Many nurses work 10 hours a day for 4 days and then have 3 days off, for example. The proportion of nurses who work part-time (28 percent) is much higher than for most occupations that require so much education and training.

The actual working conditions of a nurse depend a great deal on the kinds of patients being cared for. Emergency rooms, nurseries, orthopedic wards, and intensive care units, for example, are very different places. All nurses, however, may suddenly be confronted with life-threatening situations.

*What you should bring to this occupation.* Nursing requires emotional stability and physical stamina. Nurses need good communication skills so that they can explain what they are doing to patients.

The educational requirements for *registered nurses* vary. Three different kinds of programs enable prospective nurses to take the required licensing exam. Programs in community colleges last about two years and lead to an associate degree. Programs run by colleges or universities last four to five years and lead to a Bachelor of Science Degree in Nursing (B.S.N.). A third type, offered by hospitals and leading to a diploma, has become less common.

While graduates of all three types of programs usually qualify for positions as staff nurses, each program has its advantages. The shortest programs are much less expensive both in terms of cost and—even more important—in terms of lost income while you are being trained. Hospital programs are often said to provide more practice working with patients. And B.S.N. degrees are required for public health nursing, admission to graduate school, and some supervisory positions. Graduates of two- and three-year programs may go back to school and earn a B.S.N., but the school may require that they retake several courses, adding to the time and expense of their education.

*The rewards.* Many nurses receive great satisfaction from helping the sick or injured become well. Their duties are not always pleasant, of course; direct patient care can be very hard work. Another difficulty with being a nurse is that not all the patients get better.

In 1998, the median salary of registered nurses was $40,690, according to the U.S. Department of Labor. Nurses receive the usual fringe benefits.

Nurses can advance in two ways: by taking on more supervisory responsibilities or by earning a graduate degree and certification that enables them to provide a higher level of nursing care, such as a nurse practitioner, nurse anesthetist, or clinical nurse.

*Where to find a job.* More than two million registered nurses were employed in 1998. Hospitals, public and private, employ about 60 percent of all nurses. Other major employers are nursing homes (most of which are privately operated), public health departments, physicians' offices, and schools.

The number of people in nursing is projected to grow in the near future. Even more jobs will become available because of turnover.

Nursing shortages exist, especially in some rural areas and in some special fields. According to the U.S. Department of Labor, job openings for nurses are expected to grow much faster than average through the year 2008.

*Where to learn more.* Information about a career as a registered nurse is available from these organizations:

American Nurses Association
600 Maryland Avenue SW
Washington, DC 20024

National League for Nursing
61 Broadway
New York, NY 10006

## Other Hospital Occupations

*Clinical laboratory technicians* are often known by their specialties; for example, they may be called medical laboratory technologists or technicians, blood-bank specialists, or biochemistry technicians. In general, these workers perform chemical and other kinds of tests on body fluids and tissues, such as the measurement of the amount of cholesterol in a blood sample. Some of these jobs require an associate's degree; others—those for technologists—require a bachelor of science degree. The median salary for clinical laboratory technicians was $32,440 in 1998, according to the Bureau of Labor Statistics. Medical laboratory technicians employed by the federal government had median annual salaries of $39,600. This is a moderate-size occupation; total employment in these fields was 313,000 in 1998. To learn more, you can contact:

American Society for Clinical Laboratory Science
7910 Woodmont Avenue, Suite 530
Bethesda, MD 20814

*Hospital administrators*—who are also known as *health services administrators*—are responsible for seeing that the medical staff has the equipment, working conditions, and personnel needed to treat the patients. Budgeting finances, hiring personnel, keeping the physical plant in shape, coordinating departments, and training the staff all come under their direction. Most hospital administrators have a master's degree in health care administration, although a bachelor's degree in business and management is sufficient for some positions. Administrators usually start as assistants. According to the U.S. Department of Labor, the median salary of medical and health service managers was $48,870 in 1998. High-level hospital administrators earned significantly more. Besides hospitals and health departments, health services administrators also work for nursing homes, clinics, health maintenance organizations, and group practices. To learn more contact:

American College of Healthcare Executives
  One North Franklin Street
  Chicago, IL 60606

*Licensed practical nurses (LPN's)* provide bedside care; they bathe patients, give massages, and change dressings. They also check the patient's vital signs—temperature, blood pressure, pulse, and respiration. Under supervision, they may administer medications. To become an LPN, you must complete a one-year training program in a vocational school or community college. Median salaries for LPN's were $26,940 in 1998, according to the U.S. Department of Labor. This is a fairly large occupation, employing nearly 700,000 workers. Major employers include hospitals, nursing homes, and physicians' offices. To learn more about this occupation contact:

National Association for Practical Nurse Education and Service, Inc.
  1400 Spring Street
  Silver Spring, MD 20910

National League for Nursing
    61 Broadway
    New York, NY 10006

*Physicians* work to prevent illness, restore health, and repair the results of injuries. Some treat the whole person, but most specialize in particular parts of the body, such as the heart or brain. They are among the most thoroughly educated workers, the course of study taking from four to ten years after college, including both medical school and residency requirements. They are also among the best paid, with an average income of more than $160,000. This is a fairly large occupation; about 577,000 doctors were working in 1998. To learn more about this occupation, contact:

American Medical Association
    515 North State Street
    Chicago, IL 60610

*Psychiatric aides* work with the mentally and emotionally ill, usually in hospitals and other health care facilities. They help patients with personal hygiene, if necessary, and encourage them to join in group or recreational activities. A high school education is preferred though not always required. Salaries are comparable to those of nurse aides, which are among the lower third for all wage earners. To learn more about this occupation contact:

National Association of Health Career Schools
    2301 Academy Drive
    Harrisburg, PA 17112

*Therapist* is a general title for a worker in the health field who helps people overcome physical or emotional difficulties. Specialties within this group are highly specific; a worker trained in one of them is not qualified to work in another one. Among the titles of job specialties are physical, occupational, speech, recreation, art, dance, music, and horticultural therapist; rehabilitation counselor;

audiologist; and orientation therapist for the blind. Some thera-
pists diagnose the person's problem and devise ways to conquer it;
others work in cooperation with a doctor who diagnoses and pre-
scribes treatment. They usually need at least a bachelor's degree in
their specialized field.

## CHAPTER 15

# ROAD CONSTRUCTION AND MAINTENANCE

Highways, streets, bridges, tunnels, and street lighting systems are built and maintained by state and local governments, even if—as is the case with the interstate system—90 percent of the money to pay for the road comes from the federal government. Civil engineers and surveyors plan the roads, construction workers—many of them heavy equipment operators—build them, construction inspectors—whose duties are described in the chapter on housing—check them while they are being built, large crews of maintenance workers keep them smooth and free of snow, and toll collectors take in some of the money to pay for them. Since much of the construction and maintenance work must be done in the summer, highway departments often hire large numbers of summer workers.

About half a million workers—a little less than 5 percent of all state and local government workers—are in this category; state governments employ about half the workers, and cities and counties divide the rest between them. Employment has been declining in this function of government. A need for major reconstruction and renovation might lead to larger highway departments, but that remains to be seen.

## CIVIL ENGINEERS

Civil engineering concerns the design of roads, bridges, and other structures. Civil engineers must determine whether the site is suitable for the structure, what materials are needed, and how much the construction will cost. They also supervise construction. Much of their time is spent writing or delivering reports and consulting with other people working on the project. Specialists within this occupation include structural engineers, highway engineers, construction engineers, hydraulic engineers, traffic engineers, and soil mechanics engineers.

Engineers generally work a forty-hour week, mostly in a comfortable office, although travel to construction sites is also necessary.

*What you should bring to this occupation.* Engineers need good math and verbal skills, and they also must work well with other people. The standard educational requirement for civil engineers is a bachelor of civil engineering degree. The course of study includes subjects such as physics, calculus, surveying, structural mechanics, and the mechanics of fluids.

*The rewards.* The turnover rate for engineers is quite low, indicating that employed engineers prefer keeping their present jobs to finding new ones.

Engineers are among the highest paid workers. In 1999, the average starting salary for civil engineers reported by the National Association of Colleges and Employers was about $36,100 for those with bachelor's degrees and $42,300 for those with master's degrees. For experienced civil engineers employed by the federal government, median earnings exceeded $64,000. Engineers have the usual fringe benefits.

*Where to find a job.* About forty-eight thousand civil engineers work for state and local governments. The major employers are highway and public works departments. Civil engineering is projected to grow faster than average.

*Where to learn more.* Career information is available from the following associations:

American Society of Civil Engineers
    1801 Alexander Bell Drive
    Reston, VA 20191

National Society of Professional Engineers
    1420 King Street
    Alexandria, VA 22314

## OTHER HIGHWAY AND CONSTRUCTION OCCUPATIONS

*Heavy equipment operators* are also known as *construction machinery operators* or *operating engineers*. They drive bulldozers, backhoes, paving machines, and other equipment. They usually have experience as construction laborers or helpers before becoming heavy equipment operators. Operators employed by state and local governments are less affected by unemployment than are most construction workers. To learn more about this occupation, contact:

International Union of Operating Engineers
    1125 Seventeenth Street NW
    Washington, DC 20036

*Highway maintenance workers* have a great many duties. Signs and lines must be painted, potholes filled, cracks patched, grass mown, and snow plowed. A high school education is usually required. This is a moderate-size occupation, employing 155,000 workers in 1998, most of them with state and local governments, which are the major employers. To learn more about this occupation, you can visit the Job Service, which has job listings and offers employment counseling. You can also contact:

American Federation of State, County and Municipal Employees
   1625 L Street NW
   Washington, DC 20036

## CHAPTER 16

# HOUSING AND COMMUNITY DEVELOPMENT

When the first European settlers landed at Jamestown, in what is now Virginia, the community's first concern was housing. Housing is still a concern of local governments, whether the government has a housing authority that builds and operates developments or simply has a building standards agency, planning commission, or zoning board. Although housing is a fairly major function of state and local government, it is a minor function in terms of employment.

## CONSTRUCTION INSPECTORS

Although what goes up must come down, construction inspectors make sure that a building will not collapse before its time. They are highly specialized, some dealing with public works and others with buildings. Public works inspectors are further categorized by special areas such as highways, streets, bridges, tunnels, dams, and sewer and water systems. Specialties within building inspection include structural, electrical, and mechanical, which concern plumbing, gas lines, and heating systems.

Inspectors usually check on a project more than once during construction to ensure that it conforms with building codes.

Inspectors keep records of their work and write reports. They usually work a standard forty-hour week, spending about half their time in the office and half at construction sites.

*What you should bring to this occupation.* Knowledge of the principles of good construction and attention to detail characterize construction inspectors. They must also know the law and be able to communicate. They must usually have experience as a contractor, supervisor, or craftperson. People who have completed an apprenticeship, studied engineering or architecture for two years, or earned an associate's degree in a relevant subject are preferred. This is not a job for beginning workers.

*The rewards.* Successful building inspectors enjoy the complexity of the work and the challenge of working with a great variety of people. The job offers more security than other construction related occupations, but it does not provide the satisfaction of actually building something.

The median salary for construction inspectors with local governments was $36,300 in 1998.

*Where to find a job.* This is a fairly small occupation, with sixty-eight thousand workers in 1998, the majority being state and local government employees. Construction inspectors usually work for the building, public works, engineering, or maintenance department of the local government. Those with the state government are most likely to be with the highway department.

Only slow growth is projected for this occupation and turnover is low. Opportunities are best in rapidly growing communities or states.

*Where to learn more.* Local governments and the following associations can provide more information about the job of construction inspector:

International Association of Electrical Inspectors
P.O. Box 830848
Richardson, TX 75083

International Conference of Building Officials
  5360 Workman Mill Road
  Whittier, CA 90601

## URBAN PLANNERS

Urban and regional planners design new or renovated developments. Also known as community or city planners, they juggle the need for housing, schools, industrial sites, business sections, and parks along with requirements for transportation, sanitation, electricity, and natural gas. They must study current conditions, consider long-term development, estimate costs, build models, present plans before authorizing boards, and supervise construction. A master's degree in planning is the usual educational requirement, although some positions require only a bachelor's degree. In 1997, average salaries for planners with local governments were $40,700; planners with state governments averaged $38,900. This is a relatively small occupation with a total employment of about thirty-five thousand; local, regional, and state government planning commissions employ about 60 percent of these workers. To learn more about this occupation, you can contact:

American Planning Association
  Education Division
  122 South Michigan Avenue
  Chicago, IL 60603

## CHAPTER 17

# LIBRARY JOBS

Librarians in public libraries usually work for local governments. Librarians almost always need a bachelor's degree and often a master's. More libraries are operated by the schools; these librarians may be required to be former teachers as well as having additional education. Many libraries also employ *library aides,* however, who do not need as much education.

## LIBRARIANS

Video cassettes, compact disks, books—today, information comes in many forms. Librarians must be familiar with them all, for their job is to make information available. Some librarians perform technical services—ordering books, cataloging material, or having sets of magazines bound for the permanent collection. Most librarians provide user services. They explain how the library is arranged, where different kinds of material are kept, and how to use machines such as microfilm and microfiche readers. The majority of librarians work in schools; teaching students how to use a library is an important part of their duties.

Librarians usually work a five-day, forty-hour week. Depending on the hours the library is open, evening or weekend work may be required. Many librarians—more than 20 percent—work part-time.

*What you should bring to this occupation.* Successful librarians are good at explaining things to a great variety of people. Librarians also need good memories for the sources of information.

Schools often prefer to hire former teachers who have taken additional education related to library science, media resources, or audiovisual communications. Public libraries prefer applicants who have earned a master of library science degree.

*The rewards.* Librarians have the satisfaction of helping people find what they need. Librarians express some dissatisfaction with their wages, which are quite low for the education required.

Librarians can advance into administrative positions, some of which require additional education. School librarians have fewer opportunities to become supervisors since there is often only one librarian in the school.

According to the U.S. Department of Labor, median earnings for librarians were $38,470 in 1998. The average for those employed by the federal government, including those in management positions who tend to earn higher salaries, was $56,400 in 1999.

*Where to find a job.* About 152,000 librarians were employed in 1998, mostly in schools and public libraries. More than 70 percent of all librarians are in the educational services sector.

The following associations have information on this career:

American Library Association
50 East Huron Street
Chicago, IL 60611

Association for Library and Information Science Education
P.O. Box 7640
Arlington, VA 22207

## LIBRARY TECHNICIANS AND AIDES

Library technicians and aides (who may also be called assistants, helpers, or clerks) perform a variety of duties that help a library run smoothly. They check books and other materials in and out, sort and shelve them, calculate fines, locate items for users, issue library cards, repair or bind materials, and provide information. Technicians have more complicated duties and less supervision than aides. Some college course work (up to two years in a program for technicians) may be required of technicians; a high school education is usually sufficient for aides. Aides with simple clerical duties receive salaries comparable to other clerical workers. To learn more about this occupation, contact:

Council on Library/Media Technology
P.O. Box 951
Oxon Hill, MD 20750

## CHAPTER 18

# NATURAL RESOURCES, PARKS, AND RECREATION

Natural resources are managed by state and local governments and by federal agencies such as the Department of Agriculture and Department of the Interior. The state agency will be called the Department of Public Resources, Department of Conservation, or other similar name. Among the functions of the state and local agencies are agricultural extension and inspection services, fish stocking, flood control, forest fire prevention and control, irrigation, land and forest reclamation, mineral resource management, and soil conservation. State and local governments are major employers. Most of the employment is at the state level, although counties and special districts also have some workers in this category. These workers include agricultural extension agents, foresters, range managers, and fish and game wardens.

Parks operated by the government range in size from small local playgrounds to vast national forests. Besides playgrounds, a park department may also run pools, public beaches, golf courses, museums, botanical gardens, and zoos, each of which needs different kinds of workers.

All parks need administrative and maintenance workers. City parks often have special programs and employ recreation workers trained to run such activities. Lifeguards, gardeners, animal keepers, and museum technicians are some of the other people who work for parks departments.

## FORESTERS

Foresters are doctors for the woods. Their goal is to ensure that the trees are healthy and protected from disease, fire, and infestations of insects. They pursue this goal in many ways, including conducting research, supervising parks, managing watersheds, replanting burned over or harvested forests, and establishing guidelines for lumbering operations. Foresters usually work eight hours a day, five days a week. Much of their work takes place in offices, but they may be required to work outside in all kinds of weather, especially if a forest fire is raging or a hiking party gets lost.

*What you should bring to this occupation.* Foresters generally have an aptitude for science and enough physical agility to make their way in the woods. A bachelor's degree in forestry is required for most entry-level positions, and a graduate degree is often preferred. The college curriculum includes courses in forest protection and silviculture; frequently, a summer camp that provides practical experience is required.

*The rewards.* Foresters receive satisfaction from working to preserve the woods or to make them more productive. Competition for these jobs has been extreme for some time, however, and relocating is often necessary to find employment.

The median earnings for foresters employed by state governments were $37,400 in 1997.

*Where to find a job.* The federal government is a major employer of foresters; many are also employed by state and local governments. Lumber companies are the principal employers of foresters outside the government.

*Where to learn more.* The following organizations can provide further information about forestry:

National Society of State Foresters
    444 North Capitol Street NW
    Washington, DC 20001

Society of American Foresters
    5400 Grosvenor Lane
    Bethesda, MD 20814

## PARK RANGERS

Park rangers are responsible for maintaining order in public parks, which involves directing traffic, providing information, and patrolling the park to prevent violations of the law or park rules. Administering first aid and assisting with disabled vehicles are common tasks.

Park rangers are outdoors in all kinds of weather. They usually work a forty-hour week, but their shifts are irregular. Since the parks are busiest on weekends and holidays, rangers are likely to work during these times.

*What you should bring to this occupation.* Park rangers must be able to keep calm in emergencies, make decisions rapidly, and remain courteous after the two hundredth repetition of the same question.

A high school education is usually required; college-level courses in recreational leadership, environmental science, psychology, sociology, and biology may be helpful.

Applicants are given a series of tests before becoming ranger trainees, including written exams, physical agility tests, medical examinations, and interviews. Rangers are trained after being hired, sometimes at a police academy.

*The rewards.* Rangers have the satisfaction of combining an interest in the outdoors with protecting people and the parks.

Rangers will most likely receive salaries comparable to those of police officers in the same area.

*Where to find a job.* The National Park Service is a major employer of rangers. In various states, agencies that employ rangers might be called any of the following names: Department of Parks, Department of Parks and Recreation, Department of Natural Resources, Department of Conservation, Department of Forests and Waters, and similar designations.

## OTHER PARKS AND RECREATION OCCUPATIONS

*Landscape architects* design gardens and parks. They determine which plants are suitable for an area, taking the soil, sunlight, water supply, and proposed use into account. They also plan the type and position of roads, walks, fences, lamps, furniture, drains, and sprinkler systems. A bachelor's degree in landscape architecture—which may take five years to complete—is usually required. In 1998, median annual earnings for landscape architects were $37,930, according to the U.S. Department of Labor. The middle 50 percent earned $28,820 to $50,550. In 1999, those employed by the federal government, including supervisors, earned more than $57,000. This is a small occupation, with about twenty-two thousand workers. The major employers in state and local government are park departments, school systems, hospitals, city planning agencies, and extension services. To learn more about this occupation, contact:

American Society of Landscape Architects
    636 Eye Street NW
    Washington, DC 20001

*Recreation workers* organize games and other activities to help people make the most of their free time. The kinds of activities they direct depend in part on the place where they work, which can range in size from a city playground to a vast forest. A bachelor's degree is usually required; for some positions, the degree must be in recreation and leisure studies or a special field such as music or art. Median earnings in this field were about $16,000 in 1998, with the middle 50 percent earning between $12,000 and $20,000 annually. This is a moderate-size occupation with a total employment of about 241,000. To learn more about this occupation, contact:

National Recreation and Park Association
  22377 Belmont Ridge Road
  Ashburn, VA 20148

## CHAPTER 19

# POSTAL WORKERS

With nearly nine-hundred thousand workers, the U.S. Postal Service is the largest single employer of government workers other than the Defense Department. Postal workers are the most widespread group of federal employees. There are thousands of post offices and other postal facilities around the country, ranging in size from the corner of a rural grocery store to the blocks-long building in New York City, where more than forty thousand workers keep the mail moving day and night. There are also hundreds of mail distribution centers. The range of jobs in the Postal Service is as great as the variety of buildings it owns or uses, but 90 percent of the white-collar workers are in just five occupations: postal clerk, mail carrier, mail handler, supervisor of the mails, and postmaster. Motor vehicle driver and maintenance workers are the largest blue-collar occupations.

## POSTAL CLERKS

Postal clerks, who number about three-hundred thousand, include distribution clerks, distribution machine clerks, and window clerks.

*Distribution clerks* sort the mail: some by airmail or surface routes; others by ZIP code, city, or region; and others by delivery route. Some distribution clerks also keep records, cancel the stamps on mail that requires special handling, and work at the public windows in the post office.

*Distribution machine clerks* run the sorting equipment that helps reduce the need for distribution clerks. They first load the machines, making sure that all the envelopes face the same way. Then, as the machines present each letter to the operators, they read the ZIP code and press a combination of keys to send the letter into its proper bin. The operator does this fifty times a minute, a task that requires sharp vision.

*Window clerks* are much more visible than the other clerks, who work behind the scenes. The window clerks sell stamps and money orders, give out mail, collect postage, listen to and act on complaints, answer questions, and explain the distinctions between first, second, third, and fourth class mail.

In 1998, postal service clerks had median annual earnings of $35,100.

## MAIL CARRIERS AND RELATED POSITIONS

The nation's 332,000 mail carriers are the last link of the chain that connects the letter writer to the letter reader. Carriers take the mail for their route and sort it in the sequence of delivery. They deliver the mail—by foot in cities, by car in rural areas—collect charges for postage and C.O.D. transactions, and pick up mail from people along their routes. Back at the post office, they re-address mail that has to be forwarded, make records of changes in addresses, and take care of other matters. One advantage of a mail carrier's job is being able to set one's own pace, so long as the last delivery is made on schedule. One disadvantage is summed up in the Postal Service motto: "Neither snow nor rain nor heat nor gloom of night stays these couriers from the swift completion of their appointed rounds."

Mail carriers had median annual salaries of $34,840 in 1998.

*Mail handlers* are not nearly so numerous as carriers and clerks, though they still comprise a sizeable work force. Mail handlers load and unload trucks, trains, and planes, move bulk mail, operate canceling machines and forklifts, and repackage torn parcels.

*Supervisors* of the mails are administrators. They oversee the task of distributing and delivering the mail. They evaluate the workloads of carriers, make assignments, recommend changes in routes, see that the proper records are kept, and make sure that service at the public windows is as good as possible.

## POSTMASTERS

Postmasters manage post offices. Their duties depend on the size of the post office of which they are in charge. Many postmasters work in very small post offices that are open for only a few hours a day. Such a post office might have window and general delivery operations and a rural delivery route—all supervised by the postmaster. In addition, the postmaster would be responsible for seeing that incoming mail was properly classified and that the proper records were kept. The postmaster's job in a city post office is much more complex. The postmaster needs many subordinates and would have to devote more time to personnel actions, planning, and management than the rural postmaster.

The Postal Service is the only agency of the federal government in which labor unions play an important part. Its hiring practices are also somewhat unusual. For the clerical and carrier positions, each post office and distribution center keeps its own list of eligible job seekers, although employment standards are set nationally.

Clerks and carriers must be at least eighteen years old. In actuality, relatively few people are hired before they are about twenty-five, because of the length of the waiting periods before and after filing applications. Many postal workers transfer from other occupations. Applicants must pass a four-part written test and show that they can handle seventy-pound mail sacks. They often start working part-time before advancing to a full-time position. Supervisors of the mails and postmasters are almost always chosen from the ranks of the clerks and carriers, since experience in the distribution and delivery of mail is a major qualification. Postmasters are not political appointees.

For more information about employment with the Postal Service, contact the personnel office of your local post office or the nearest mail distribution center. They are the only places where you can find out when the employment tests are given and how to register for them. Applications are accepted *only* when the post office decides that a test must be given; therefore, you might need to keep checking back before you actually file an application. The tests are given no more often than once every year or two, and it may take as long as two years before someone who passed the test is hired.

## CHAPTER 20

# SANITATION, TRANSPORTATION, AND UTILITIES

Sanitation is generally the responsibility of the local government, although often, especially in smaller communities, the government contracts with a private company for sanitation services. Sanitation departments employ workers to drive trucks, collect refuse, and perform other duties. The largest occupation in these departments is sanitation workers.

## SANITATION WORKERS

When asked how business was, the sanitation worker replied cheerfully, "It's picking up." Sanitation workers pick up refuse from homes and businesses and burn it or use it for landfill. Jobs include refuse collector, truck driver, incinerator operator, and landfill operator. Many sanitation workers start as refuse collectors either emptying trash cans into a truck or operating special trucks that pick up larger bins and dumpsters.

The standard workweek is forty hours. Sanitation workers are outside in all kinds of weather, both winter ice and summer heat, making their job more difficult.

*What you should bring to this occupation.* Sanitation workers should enjoy physical labor and working outside, since lifting heavy cans and walking much of the day is their major job. A high school education is usually required, and applicants may have to be licensed drivers.

*The rewards.* No one is likely to consider sanitation work a glamorous job; the work must be done, however, and sanitation workers are proud of the contribution they make to the health of their communities.

Sanitation workers start as laborers and can advance to driver and then to supervisory positions.

## TRANSPORTATION

Public mass transportation systems include subways, surface railroads, and bus systems. Bus driver is the largest single transit occupation.

### Bus Drivers

Through rain and snow and gloom of night—not to mention traffic jams—bus drivers daily carry millions of people, mostly schoolchildren. Drivers inspect the bus before starting, checking such things as safety equipment, fuel supply, and brakes. They follow a specified schedule, being careful not to be early or late. Local transit bus drivers also collect fares, issue transfers, and provide route information. Bus drivers also must be able to make out route and accident reports.

A very large number of bus drivers—45 percent—work part-time. School bus drivers usually work twenty to thirty hours a week. The standard workweek for local transit bus drivers is forty hours; however, split shifts, in which the driver is on duty for both the morning and evening rush hours with several hours off in between, are common. Weekend work is also required of local transit bus drivers.

Working conditions for drivers largely depend on the weather, even though the bus provides protection from the elements.

*What you should bring to this occupation.* Bus drivers should like working with people and being independent at the same time. They should have the patience to deal with noisy children and traffic delays. They should speak well enough to answer a rider's questions.

Applicants should have a driver's license; a chauffeur's license is usually required to drive a bus, but you may be able to obtain the license after being hired. You should learn the policy of the company or transportation authority you wish to work for before applying.

A driving test and a medical examination may be required. Some states require a background check of school bus drivers to ensure that applicants do not have a history of emotional instability.

After being hired, drivers are trained for two to eight weeks in practical driver training, traffic laws, and bus company regulations.

*The rewards.* Successful bus drivers enjoy driving and like being outside and moving around. The job can be stressful, however; opportunities for promotion are limited, and seasonal layoffs may be routine. Drivers may become dispatchers, but few other opportunities for advancement are available.

The median hourly wage for school bus drivers was $9.05 in 1998, according to the U.S. Department of Labor. Transit and intercity drivers average $11.72 per hour.

*Where to find a job.* The number of bus drivers—638,000—is very large. The majority drive school buses, while others drive for transit systems or other employers.

*Where to learn more.* For more information, contact:

American Bus Association
  1100 New York Avenue NW
  Washington, DC 20005

National School Transportation Association
    P.O. Box 2639
    Springfield, VA 22152

General information on local transit bus driving is available from:

American Public Transit Association
    1201 New York Avenue NW, Ste. 400
    Washington, DC 20005

## WATER AND WASTEWATER TREATMENT PLANT OPERATORS

Part mechanic and part technician, these workers operate pumps, adjust valves, inspect pipes and other equipment, check gauges, and adjust controls. They take water samples and test them chemically or perform biological analyses. They make minor repairs to equipment. In larger plants, operators are more specialized, performing only one function; but in small plants, they do everything.

Water treatment plant operators usually work a forty-hour week; weekend and night hours are required, however, since most plants operate around the clock. Operators move around in their work, climbing ladders and scrambling over pipes.

*What you should bring to this occupation.* Successful operators enjoy working with machinery. They should be agile enough to make their way around a plant and able to use wrenches and other hand tools. Chemical dust can cause trouble for operators with allergies.

A high school education is usually required. Applicants are tested for general intelligence, skill in elementary mathematics, and mechanical aptitude.

*The rewards.* Operators who enjoy working with machinery are most likely to find this job satisfying. The work environment can be a drawback because of noise and air pollution.

Advancement possibilities depend on the size of the plant. Larger plants usually offer more opportunities; the top jobs at larger plants, however, may require a college degree in engineering or science.

Water treatment plant operators earned median annual salaries of $29,960 in 1998. Workers in larger plants, with more complicated jobs or with supervisory responsibilities, earned more. Operators received the usual fringe benefits.

*Where to find a job.* About ninety-eight thousand water and sewage plant operators were employed in 1998. Water, sewage, and pollution control departments are the most likely employers.

*Where to learn more.* Local employers are the best source of information about this occupation.

# WELFARE AND HUMAN SERVICES

Public welfare departments administer programs such as Aid to Families with Dependent Children, Food Stamps, and Medicaid. They also may provide social services like day care, counseling, and homemaker services. In addition to administrative and clerical workers—notably claims clerks—welfare departments employ thousands of social workers.

Social insurance administration and employment services have become government functions only in this century. The states administer unemployment insurance programs and worker's compensation programs and provide job counseling and job training. They also run the states' Job Services, which function like a state employment agency. Job Service employees interview applicants to determine their skills and interests, find employers with vacancies, and match the applicants with the openings.

## SOCIAL WORKERS

Meeting some of the needs caused by poverty and disadvantage is the social worker's goal. Social caseworkers meet with individuals, families, or groups, try to identify what problems the people have, and suggest ways to solve them. Some temporary solutions are fairly simple. For example, if a family has no money because the adults are unable to work, the social worker can arrange for welfare payments to be made. Many problems are much more complex—drug addiction, for example. In these cases, social workers may refer the clients to other specialists and programs. They are trained to recognize that many people with such severe problems may need more intensive and specialized care. Caseworkers are also trained in knowing how and where to refer people for special care, and in coordinating the services of different agencies. Most social workers are caseworkers—that is, they work directly with those in need—but some are administrators, teachers, or researchers.

Social workers may specialize in particular fields. About half of all social workers are in just three categories: mental health, child/youth, and medical/health. Similar work is performed by probation and parole officers, whose occupations are described in Chapter 10.

Social workers usually have an eight-hour day, five days a week. Much of their time is spent in offices, but they also may visit clients.

*What you should bring to this occupation.* Successful social workers have the sensitivity to care for the needy and the maturity to face trying conditions. They make independent decisions at the same time that they accept the rules of their agency.

The usual educational requirement is a bachelor's degree in social work, psychology, or sociology. Some positions require a master of social work degree (M.S.W.).

More than half the states require that social workers be licensed.

*The rewards.* Social workers have the satisfaction of helping people in need. Among the frustrations of the job are the relatively low wages—considering the education required—the difficulty of working with government agencies, and the apparent hopelessness of the situation: that needs are unlimited, and resources are limited.

Social workers may advance to supervisory positions or enter teaching. Further education may be necessary for advancement.

Social workers receive the usual fringe benefits. In 1998, median annual earnings for social workers were $30,590. For those employed by the federal government, the median salary exceeded $45,000.

*Where to find a job.* About six-hundred thousand social workers were employed in 1998. State and local governments are major employers along with hospitals, social service agencies, educational agencies, and other employers.

*Where to learn more.* The following associations can provide further information:

Council on Social Work Education
    1600 Duke Street
    Alexandria, VA 22314

National Association of Social Workers
    750 First Street NE
    Washington, DC 20002

## CHAPTER 22

# PLANNING FOR TOMORROW

You would not be reading these words if you were not either preparing to train for a career *or* preparing to change careers. Your final decision may be affected by what you read in the coming pages. It is also possible that you will evaluate all the facts you can muster and still decide to enter an occupation that does not make anyone's "fastest growing" list. The decision, while yours alone, should be an informed one. If you want to spend your life in the wild as a forest ranger, then do it happily—although armed in advance with the facts about salary, working conditions, and outlook for growth. If you yearn for a six-figure paycheck, by all means consider the outlook for those jobs that will provide one.

## WHERE WILL THE JOBS COME FROM?

The majority of jobs in the near future will result from replacement needs. Even jobs with slow growth potential will be available as people who hold them retire, return to school, assume household responsibilities, or, in the case of federal, state, and local government, leave for jobs in the private sector.

The jobs with the highest replacement levels are in those occupations that are large, have low pay and status, low training requirements, and a high proportion of young and part-time workers.

The occupations with relatively few replacement openings are those with high pay and status, long training requirements, and a high proportion of full-time workers.

Other jobs will open up in large numbers in those categories that show faster than average growth. The *Occupational Outlook Handbook,* published by the U.S. Department of Labor, is a good source of information about job trends. It provides details about hundreds of jobs and includes sections on: the nature of the work, working conditions, number of people employed, training, other qualifications and chances for advancement, job outlook, earnings, related occupations, and sources of even more information. Please note that this is information for *all* jobs, both public and private. It will often tell you, however, how many of the total labor force are employed in the public sector. The *Handbook* can be purchased from the U.S. Department of Labor or from VGM Career Books, Lincolnwood, IL. It is also available in most public and school libraries.

As we continue to shift from the Industrial Age to the Age of Information, from goods-producing to service-producing employment, we often question whether there will even *be* jobs for us in the future. The answer, as we can see, is that there will be jobs—more and more of them. As has been said many times, however, we may need to stay flexible, keep learning, and be more and more responsible for our futures. We will have to learn to be lifelong students; we will have to know where the jobs are and where the jobs *will be.* We also will have to know where and how to prepare for changing job markets. We need to remember that most of the jobs in the future will require a good bit of education. The jobs that used to go to high school dropouts and the minimally literate are the jobs that are disappearing. The job of the future must be filled by specially trained people who also are able to read and follow directions carefully. New technologies are, after all, only as good as the workers who are skilled in their use.

## CHOOSING AND PREPARING FOR AN OCCUPATION

This book should make it obvious that governments offer a great range of employment opportunities. It is up to you to learn which ones suit you best. You will have to learn about the federal government as well as your own state and neighboring states, your own local government and neighboring ones. You will have to decide which occupations appeal to you and then find out what qualifications these various governments demand and what benefits they offer. The sooner you do so, the better. You don't want to wait until the last minute only to find out that the examination you need to take was just offered and won't be given again for another year.

You should begin the process of choosing an occupation by analyzing yourself. Ask what you have—interests, skills, talents, physical conditions, work history, and education. Ask what you want: Money? Prestige? Adventure? To help others? To live in a certain place? To work on a team? Indoors? Part-time? Then explore careers, to find one that will most closely match what you want to do.

Career guidance and occupational information is provided in many books, several of which are listed in Appendix A. Counseling to help you determine which occupations you are best prepared for may also be available. Surfing the Internet is another way to obtain career information. You'll also want to talk to people who actually have the kind of job you want. In many cases, they can point out things that books don't mention or make seem unimportant. One of the best ways to learn how much you like a job is to try it out through seasonal, part-time, or volunteer work.

Preparing for an occupation can be very expensive. Therefore, you want to be as certain as possible that the job is for you and that there will be a job for you. National outlook information is given throughout this book. For many people, however, the local outlook is much more important. It is also harder to determine. You can obtain some information from the state Job Service: The address of the office nearest you will be listed in the state government section of the telephone book. You can also contact potential employers and people now working in a field to ask how the future looks. Such a step is especially important before you commit yourself to an expensive educational program. Ask the school to give you the names of graduates now working in the occupation. Contact the graduates and ask if the schooling was worthwhile. Also contact their employers to learn if the particular school's program is highly thought of, or if it played no part in the decision to hire the graduate. You can also contact the Better Business Bureau to learn if there are any complaints about the school. A school that will not provide references—and one that promises you a job—should be treated with suspicion. For information on education and training programs, check a public library or school library. Talk to the librarians and gather as much information as you can before making a decision.

# FURTHER READING

Carland, Maria Pinto and Michael Trucano, Editors. *Careers in International Affairs.* Washington, DC: Georgetown University Press, 1996.

Damp, Dennis. *The Book of U.S. Government Jobs: Where They Are, What's Available and How to Get One.* Moon Township, PA: Brookhaven Press, 2000.

Douglas, John E. *John Douglas' Guide to Careers in the FBI.* New York: Simon and Schuster, 1998.

Grey, Lawrence. *How to Win a Local Election: A Complete Step-by-Step Guide.* Albuquerque, NM: National Book Network, 1999.

Guber, Susan. *How to Win Your 1st Election: The Candidate's Handbook.* Boca Raton, FL: CRC Press, 1999.

Krannich, Ronald. *Find a Federal Job Fast!* Manassas Park, VA: Impact Publications, 1998.

Learning Express. *Civil Service Career Starter.* New York: LearningExpress, 2000.

McKiney, Anne, Editor. *Government Job Applications and Federal Resumes.* Fayetteville, NC: Prep Publishing, 1999.

Morgan, Dana and Dana Goldenkoff. *Federal Jobs: The Ultimate Guide.* Indianapolis, IN: IDG Books, 1996.

Pitz, Mary Elisabeth. *Careers in Government.* Lincolnwood, IL: VGM Career Books, 1999.

Wood, Patricia B. and Michelle Macie. *Applying for Federal Jobs: A Guide to Writing Successful Applications and Resumes for the Job You Want in Government.* Moon Township, PA: Brookhaven Press, 1995.

# APPENDIX B

# ASSOCIATIONS

Many associations provide a wealth of information to job seekers. Three types of information will probably be most useful: career guidance material in either books or pamphlets; periodicals that contain position announcements, want ads, or articles about new developments in the field; and directories of members—which you can use to find local people to talk to about an occupation. Besides the associations listed elsewhere in this book, many other associations are listed in the *Encyclopedia of Associations,* an annual 3-volume publication, available in most libraries. Section 3 of the *Encyclopedia* lists associations in government and public administration; the other sections of the *Encyclopedia* list thousands of occupational associations. Many associations also maintain websites that can be accessed through a standard Internet search.

# FEDERAL JOB INFORMATION CENTERS

## Alabama

520 Wynn Drive NW
Huntsville, AL 35816-3426
24-hour telephone service: (205) 837-0894

## Alaska

222 West Seventh Avenue, #22, Room 156
Anchorage, AK 99513-7572
Callers in Alaska: (907) 271-5821
Callers outside Alaska: (912) 757-3000

## Arizona

See New Mexico

## Arkansas

See San Antonio, TX

## California

9650 Flair Drive, Suite 100A
El Monte, CA 91731
24-hour telephone service: (818) 575-6510

1029 J Street, Room 202
Sacramento, CA 95814
24-hour telephone service: (415) 744-5627
Self-service: M–F/8–4

Federal Building, Room 4260
880 Front Street
San Diego, CA 92101
24-hour telephone service: (818) 575-6510
Self-service: M–F/8–5

120 Howard Street, Suite B
For mail only: P.O. Box 7405
San Francisco, CA 94120
24-hour telephone service: (415) 744-5627

## Colorado
12345 West Alameda Parkway
For mail only: P.O. Box 25167
Lakewood, CO 80225
24-hour telephone service: (303) 969-7050

## Connecticut
See Boston, MA

## Delaware
See Philadelphia, PA

## District of Columbia
Theodore Roosevelt Federal Building
1900 E Street NW, Room 1416
Washington, DC 20415

**Florida**
    See Georgia

**Georgia**
    Richard B. Russell Federal Building, Room 940A
    75 Spring Street SW
    Atlanta, GA 30303
    24-hour telephone service: (404) 331-4315

**Hawaii**
    Federal Building, Room 5316
    300 Ala Moana Boulevard
    Honolulu, HI 96850
    Callers in Hawaii: 24-hour telephone service (808) 541-2791
    Callers outside Hawaii: (912) 757-3000

**Idaho**
    See Seattle, WA

**Illinois**
    230 South Dearborn Street, Room 2916
    Chicago, IL 60604
    24-hour telephone service: (312) 353-6192
    For Madison and St. Clair counties, see St. Louis, MO

**Indiana**
    See Michigan
    For Clark, Dearborn, and Floyd counties, see Ohio

**Iowa**
    See Kansas City, MO
    For Scott County, see Illinois

**Kansas**
See Kansas City, MO

**Kentucky**
See Ohio
For Henderson County, see Michigan

**Louisiana**
See San Antonio, TX

**Maine**
See Boston, MA

**Maryland**
See Philadelphia, PA

**Massachusetts**
Thos. P. O'Neill, Jr., Federal Building
10 Causeway Street
Boston, MA 02222
24-hour telephone service: (617) 565-5900

**Michigan**
477 Michigan Avenue, Room 565
Detroit, MI 48226
24-hour telephone service: (313) 226-6950

**Minnesota**
Bishop Henry Whipple Federal Building
1 Federal Drive, Room 501
Ft. Snelling, MN 55111
24-hour telephone service: (612) 725-3430

**Mississippi**
See Alabama

**Missouri**
Federal Building, Room 134
601 East Twelfth Street
Kansas City, MO 64106
24-hour telephone service: (816) 426-5702
For counties west of and including Mercer, Grundy, Carroll,
Livingston, Saline, Pettis, Benton, Hickory, Dallas, Webster,
Douglas, and Ozark

400 Old Post Office Building
815 Olive Street
St. Louis, MO 63101
24-hour telephone service: (314) 539-2285
For all other Missouri counties not listed under Kansas City
above

**Montana**
See Colorado

**Nebraska**
See Kansas City, MO

**Nevada**
For Clark, Lincoln, and Nye counties, see Los Angeles, CA
For all other Nevada counties not listed above, see Sacramento,
CA

**New Hampshire**
See Boston, MA

**New Jersey**
>   For Bergen, Essex, Hudson, Hunterdon, Middlesex, Morris,
>   Passaic, Somerset, Sussex, Union, and Warren counties, see
>   New York City, NY

>   For Atlantic, Burlington, Camden, Cape May, Cumberland,
>   Gloucester, Mercer, Monmouth, Ocean, and Salem counties,
>   see Philadelphia, PA

**New Mexico**
>   505 Marquette Avenue, Suite 910
>   Albuquerque, NM 87102
>   24-hour telephone service: (505) 766-5583

**New York**
>   Jacob K. Javits Federal Building
>   30th Floor, Room 3036
>   26 Federal Plaza
>   New York, NY 10278
>   (212) 264-0422/0423

>   James M. Hanley Federal Building
>   100 South Clinton Street, Room 841
>   P.O. Box 7257
>   Syracuse, NY 13261
>   24-hour telephone service: (315) 448-0480

**North Carolina**
>   4407 Bland Road, Suite 202
>   Raleigh, NC 27609
>   24-hour telephone service: (919) 790-2822

**North Dakota**
>   See Minnesota

**Ohio**
Federal Building, Room 506
200 West Second Street
Dayton, OH 45402
24-hour telephone service: (513) 225-2720
For Van Wert, Auglaize, Hardin, Marion, Crawford, Richland,
   Ashland, Wayne, Stark, Carroll, Columbiana counties and
   farther north, see Michigan

**Oklahoma**
See San Antonio, TX

**Oregon**
Federal Building, Room 376
1220 SW Third Avenue
Portland, OR 97204
24-hour telephone service: (503) 326-3141

**Pennsylvania**
Wm. J. Green, Jr., Federal Building
600 Arch Street
Philadelphia, PA 19106
24-hour telephone service: (215) 597-7440

**Puerto Rico**
U.S. Federal Building, Room 328
150 Carlos Chardon Avenue
San Juan 00918
(809) 766-5242

**Rhode Island**
See Boston, MA

**South Carolina**
    See Raleigh, NC

**South Dakota**
    See Minnesota

**Tennessee**
    See Alabama

**Texas**
    Corpus Christi
    See San Antonio
    (512) 884-8113

    Dallas
    See San Antonio

    Harlingen
    See San Antonio
    (512) 412-0722

    Houston
    See San Antonio
    (713) 759-0455

    8610 Broadway, Room 305
    San Antonio, TX 78217
    (210) 805-2423
    For forms call: (210) 805-2406

**Utah**
    See Colorado

**Vermont**
    See Boston, MA

**Virgin Islands**
See Puerto Rico (809) 774-8790

**Virginia**
For mail only: Federal Building, Room 500
200 Granby Street
Norfolk, VA 23510
Telephone service: (804) 441-3355
For walk-in only:
Virginia Employment Commission
5145 East Virginia Beach Boulevard, 2nd Floor

**Washington**
Federal Building, Room 110
915 Second Avenue
Seattle, WA 98174
24-hour telephone service: (206) 220-6400

**Washington, DC**
See District of Columbia

**West Virginia**
See Ohio

**Wisconsin**
For Dane, Grant, Green, Iowa, Lafayette, Jefferson, Walworth,
Milwaukee, Racine, Waukesha, Rock, and Kenosha counties,
see Illinois
For all other counties not listed above, see Minnesota

**Wyoming**
See Colorado

# COMMONLY USED U.S. OFFICE OF PERSONNEL MANAGEMENT FORMS

These forms may be obtained in "hard copy" or on-line from www.opm.gov.

**SF 15** Application for Veteran's Preference

**SF 39** Request for Referral of Eligibles

**SF 50** Notification of Personnel Action

**SF 52** Request for Personnel Action

**SF 59** Request for Approval of Non-Competitive Action

**SF 61** Appointment Affidavits

**SF 62** Agency Request to Pass Over a Preference Eligible or Object to an Eligible

**SF 71** Request for Leave or Approved Absence

**SF 75** Request for Preliminary Employment Data

**SF 85** Questionnaire for Non-Sensitive Positions

**SF 85P** Questionnaire for Public Trust Positions

**SF 85P-S** Supplemental Questionnaire for Selected Positions

**SF 86** Questionnaire for National Security Positions

**SF 86A** Continuation Sheet for Questionnaires SF 86, SF 85P, and SF 85

**SF-113A** Monthly Report of Federal Civilian Employment

**SF 181** Race and National Origin Identification (for use with current federal employees only)

**SF 256** Self-Identification of Reportable Handicap

**SF 813** Verification of a Military Retiree's Service in Non-Wartime Campaigns or Expeditions

**SF 1152** Designation of Beneficiary—Unpaid Compensation of Deceased Civilian Employee

**SF 1187** Request for Payroll Deductions for Labor Organization Dues

**SF 2800** Application for Death Benefits, CSRS

**SF 2803** Application to Make Deposit or Redeposit

**SF 2804** Application to Make Voluntary Contributions, CSRS

**SF 2804a** Information Regarding Voluntary Contributions, CSRS

**SF 2806** Individual Retirement Record

**SF 2807** Register of Separations and Transfers, CSRS

**SF 2808** Designation of Beneficiary, CSRS

**SF 2809** Employee Health Benefits Registration Form

**SF 2809–1** Annuitant/OWCP Health Benefits Registration Form

**SF 2817** Life Insurance Election: Federal Employees' Group Life Insurance Program

**SF 2818** Continuation of Life Insurance as a Retiree or Compensationer

**SF 2819** Notice of Conversion Privilege, Federal Employee's Group Life Insurance Program

**SF 2820** Certification of Insured Employee's Retired Status

**SF 2822** Request for Insurance

**SF 2823** Designation of Beneficiary, Federal Employees' Group Life Insurance Program

**SF 3102** Designation of Beneficiary, Federal Employees Retirement System

**SF 3104** Application for Death Benefit (FERS)

**SF 3104B** Documentation and Elections in Support of Application for Death Benefits when Deceased was an Employee at the Time of Death (FERS)

**SF 3106** Application for Refund of Retirement Deductions (FERS)

**SF 3106A** Current/Former Spouse's Notification of Application for Refund of Retirement Deductions Under the Federal Employees Retirement System

**SF 3109** Election of Coverage, Federal Employees Retirement System

**SF 3110** Former Spouse's Consent to FERS Election

**SF 3111** Request for Waiver, Extension, or Search in Connection with Election of FERS Coverage, Federal Employees Retirement System